Parliament today

Politics today

Series editor: Bill Jones

Forthcoming, to include:

Of related interest

Parliament today

Andrew Adonis

Manchester University Press

Manchester and New York

Distributed exclusively in the USA and Canada by St. Martin's Press

Copyright © Andrew Adonis 1990

Published by Manchester University Press
Oxford Road, Manchester M13 9PL, UK
and Room 400, 175 Fifth Avenue,
New York, NY 10010, USA

Distributed exclusively in the USA and Canada
by St. Martin's Press, Inc.,
175 Fifth Avenue, New York, NY 10010, USA

British Library cataloguing in publication data
Adonis, Andrew
    Parliament today.
    1. Great Britain. Parliament
    I. Title
    328.41

Library of Congress cataloging in publication data
Adonis, Andrew, 1963–
    Parliament today / Andrew Adonis.
      p. cm. – (Politics today)
    Includes bibliographical references.
    ISBN 0-7190-3082-X. – ISBN 0-7190-3083-8 (pbk.)
    1. Great Britain. Parliament.   I. Title.   II. Series: Politics
    today (Manchester, England)
    JN550   1990
    328.41'072 – dc20   90-5563

ISBN 0 7190 3082 X *hardback*
     0 7190 3083 8 *paperback*

Phototypeset in Great Britain
by Williams Graphics, Llanddulas, North Wales

Printed in Great Britain
by Biddles Ltd, Guildford and King's Lynn

Contents

Preface

This book is written primarily for students and general readers. It provides an up-to-date survey of Parliament at work, and highlights the political and scholarly debates on the working and effectiveness of the two Houses and their members. It is not, however, simply a digest of the relevant facts and literature. A number of fresh interpretations are put forward, and the concluding chapter can be read on its own as an essay on the 'state of Parliament' at the start of the 1990s.

I have amassed numerous debts in the preparation of the book. The greatest is to Caroline White, who gave invaluable help with the research and was a constant and candid critic of successive drafts. Michael Hart, Kathryn Davies and Benedict Grey read and improved the manuscript. Martin Horwood drew the plans of the two chambers. Richard Purslow at MUP was a source of encouragement and advice throughout. MORI kindly gave permission to publish copyright material. To these and others I am grateful; all errors and shortcomings are, of course, my responsibility alone.

A.A.
5 January 1990

Tables and figures

Tables

Figures

1
Parliament

In *Representative Government* (1861) John Stuart Mill holds up as the 'ideally best form of government' one in which ultimate power resides with the whole body of citizens. 'But', he continues, 'since all cannot, in a community exceeding a small single town, participate personally in any but some minor portions of the public business, it follows that the ideal type of a perfect government must be representative.' That is the pre-eminent justification for representative institutions in general and for the foremost of them in Britain – Parliament.

This may seem obvious today, but it has not long been so. Liberal democratic principles, a product of the great seventeenth and eighteenth-century revolutions in England, America and France, were thereafter accepted only gradually – not least in those three countries themselves. In Britain, Parliament had been in existence for centuries, and by the 1690s was an integral part of the governing process. But for another century and more Parliament remained essentially what it had been since the Middle Ages: a meeting of estates of notables, not a body representing individuals *per se*. Moreover, despite it being generally accepted that the King's government should be run by, and responsive to, the notables (still landed aristocrats for the most part), there existed only a rudimentary concept of executive (i.e. governmental) accountability to Parliament. The growth of 'popular' notions of representation and accountability was a slow and fraught affair, stimulated by the rapid urban and industrial expansion of the late eighteenth and nineteenth centuries. Contemporaries, at least, had no doubt that the turning-point was the Great Reform Act of 1832, the first statute intended to engineer a systematic overhaul of Parliament's representative credentials.

Not that the House of Commons became the handmaiden of

democracy overnight. The Great Reform Act was intended, in the words of its patron, Earl Grey, 'to give to the nation contentment, and to all future governments the support of the respectability, the wealth, and the intelligence of the country'. But once the dynamic had been set in train, political rights could not long be confined to an élite; and the next hundred years saw a succession of reform statutes, notably measures extending the right to vote in 1867, 1884, 1918 and 1928 (by when virtually all men and women were able to vote at the age of twenty-one – reduced to eighteen in 1969). Meanwhile, governments came to be formally and fully 'responsible' to the House of Commons as the popularly elected branch of Parliament. The Commons and the executive committee it sustained – the Cabinet – were now clearly, in Bagehot's celebrated *English Constitution* (1867), the 'efficient' organs of government, with the Monarchy relegated to an essentially 'dignified' role and the House of Lords somewhere between the two.

For more than a century, therefore, Britain has considered itself a democracy; and in that time its representative system has remained substantially unchanged. On the face of it, the system is simple and straightforward. The nation is divided into geographical units (*constituencies*), the voters (or *electorate*) in each of which choose a representative (a *Member of Parliament* or *MP*) from among candidates offering themselves in polls held simultaneously across all constituencies at least once every five years (a *general election*). The House of Commons thus elected is legally the supreme, or *sovereign*, power in the United Kingdom. To stand a realistic chance of election, a candidate must be nominated by a political party equipped with organisation, money and substantial popular support. Once elected, the House of Commons almost invariably entrusts executive responsibility to the party with most MPs, whose leader becomes Prime Minister and in turn appoints the Cabinet and other ministers; and the government so formed remains in office for as long as it enjoys the support (or *confidence*) of the Commons. All the while, Parliament deliberates on the proposed laws (*legislation*) of the government. It also, led by MPs outside the government, acts to make the Cabinet continually and publicly accountable for its decisions and policies.

That, of course, is an idiot's guide. In reality, the workings of Parliament are complex and untidy, like those of government, elections and party politics with which they are intimately bound up. This book aims to make them intelligible and to give an up-to-date picture of Parliament at work. However, some prior understanding of

Parliament's structure, history and place in the wider political and social life of contemporary Britain is essential. The rest of this chapter therefore briefly describes Parliament's development, and introduces the activities and institutions which form the basis of the following chapters.

The Queen-in-Parliament

Parliament – or, properly speaking, 'the Queen-in-Parliament' – is made up of three separate branches: the Sovereign, the House of Lords and the House of Commons. Nowadays the three assemble together only once a year, for the State Opening of Parliament at the start of each new parliamentary *session*.* At the State Opening, the Queen, crowned and in regal apparel, from the throne in the House of Lords with the peers before her in ermine robes and the Commons at the Bar, delivers a 'Gracious Speech' outlining the policies and programme of 'My Government' for the coming year. It is an awesome spectacle, but now entirely ceremonial – even the Gracious Speech is written by the Prime Minister. The Monarch has a few other parliamentary functions besides conducting the State Opening, but they now have practically no bearing on the work of the two Houses. Symbolically, for all but one day of the year the throne is draped in satin and separated from the Lords by a brass rail.

Nonetheless, to understand Parliament it is essential to understand that it is fundamentally a royal creation. Its name derives from the Latin word *parliamentum*, first used in medieval England to denote a formal council of the 'great men' summoned periodically by the King, in the words of the Provisions of Oxford (1258), 'to view the state of the kingdom and to treat of the common business of the kingdom and of the king likewise'. The composition of these 'parliaments' was subsequently formalised, as the two 'Houses' – of Lords (the great lay and ecclesiastical magnates) and Commons (gentry for the most part, chosen by the wealthy of the shires and boroughs) – began to sit apart, and as the need for parliamentary consent to new taxes and laws came to be accepted. MPs were not always content to do the King's bidding: they could be troublesome, and engaged in frequent criticism

* The interval between general elections is called a *parliament* and is divided into legislative terms (*sessions*), each lasting about a year. Sessions usually start and finish in mid-November, although they are upset by general elections.

of royal officials – whom they sometimes even sought to remove or impeach. Even so, Parliament remained a royal institution, summoned by the King, deliberating on his business, bringing grievances to his notice and looking to him for remedies. As Henry VIII declared, after a fracas with the Commons in 1544: 'we at no time stand so high in our estate royal as in the time of Parliament'.

It was the Commons' attempt to invade the 'estate royal' a century later, and virtually take over the government from Charles I, that provoked the Civil War. 'In this kingdom', Charles bluntly replied to parliamentary demands, 'the government ... is entrusted to the King': the Commons, 'an excellent convener of liberty, [was] never intended for any share in government, or the choosing of them that govern.' But Charles lost the war, and after his execution in 1649 the Monarchy was abolished by Cromwell. Eleven years later it was restored, but Charles's successors – particularly those reigning after the 'Glorious Revolution' of 1688 – were obliged to take heed of the Lords and Commons in the 'choosing of them that govern'. By the reign of Queen Victoria (1837–1901) the Sovereign had all but abdicated from personal participation in administration, reserving only Bagehot's trio of privileges – 'the right to be consulted, the right to encourage, the right to warn'. ('And a king of great sense and sagacity would want no others.') The Monarch remained Head of State, while the Prime Minister, entirely dependent for office on the House of Commons, came to be recognised as the undisputed Head of Government.

However, it is important to appreciate what did *not* happen during the transition to democracy and responsible government. The Monarch's withdrawal from government led neither to the transfer of the Crown's executive role and powers to the Commons, nor to its replacement by a directly elected executive on the model of the American presidency. Rather, the Crown's governmental functions and *prerogatives** passed almost entire to the Cabinet, or in some cases directly to a particular minister. The label 'Her Majesty's Government' is thus no quaint anachronism, for it identifies the executive as more than simply an outgrowth of Parliament. Certainly, no government can long survive without the support of a Commons majority, from which it also derives most of its personnel and legislative authority,

---

* The *royal prerogative* is, historically, 'the residue of discretionary or arbitrary authority left in the hands of the Crown' (Dicey). Today the term *prerogative* is taken to refer to the discretionary powers of government, for whose exercise ministers do not require parliamentary approval.

But once formed, the Cabinet draws on a range of powers which it exercises on its own authority: some of them − like the conduct of foreign affairs − under the critical eye (but not sanction) of MPs; others − like the prerogatives of pardon, appointment and *dissolution** (the latter two in the hands on the Prime Minister alone) wielded without reference to Parliament at all.

Some go further and allege that the Cabinet has, in turn, been usurped by the Prime Minister. Whatever the validity of the claim − and in practice prime-ministerial power varies greatly from government to government − any such development is less the product of further constitutional evolution than of the dominance achieved by particular party leaders over their followers and colleagues. Bagehot's insight still holds: the Cabinet is the 'efficient secret', 'a *hyphen* which joins, a *buckle* which fastens, the legislative part of the State to the executive part of the State'.

A unitary state and sovereign parliament

Hand in hand with the rise of democracy and 'responsible government' came two other critical developments: the creation of a unitary state and the establishment of parliamentary sovereignty within it.

A unitary state
The United Kingdom, like its Parliament, is a piecemeal creation. An English state can be traced back to Alfred the Great in the ninth century. But in-fighting between royal and noble clans (from home and abroad) was endemic until the late Middle Ages. Even thereafter, the threat of rebellion against the English Crown remained potent until the suppression of the 1745 Jacobite rising, and in Ireland until the 1798 rebellion was put down. For dynastic and security reasons, therefore, successive English monarchs and parliaments sought to bring their northern and western neighbours into a subordinate relationship, and between the mid-sixteenth and late-eighteenth centuries Wales (1543), Scotland (1707) and Ireland (1800) were 'united' (as it was euphemistically termed) with England − to the end, in the words of the Act of Union with Scotland, that 'the whole Island is thereby subject to

* A *dissolution* is, in effect, the calling of a general election − so termed because the Queen formally 'dissolves' Parliament and issues a royal proclamation calling elections for a new one.

One Sovereignty and represented by One Parliament'. In each case, the King of England was already Monarch of the country in question; 'union' involved the abolition of its separate Parliament and the granting of an agreed number of MPs and peers at London in exchange.

By the Victorian era the union went largely unchallenged in Scotland and Wales; but not in Ireland, the most recent addition, where religious and economic bitterness exacerbated nationalist opposition to the Act of Union. A century of sometimes constitutional, sometimes violent struggle ensued, led by charismatic nationalists of the stamp of Daniel O'Connell, Charles Stewart Parnell and Eamon de Valera. In the 1880s Gladstone tried to stem the separatist tide by advocating the establishment of a subordinate Parliament for Ireland within the United Kingdom. 'The concession of local self-government', he told the Commons, 'is not the way to sap or impair, but the way to strengthen and consolidate unity.' But his two attempts at passing 'home rule' through Parliament failed, and it was another thirty-five years before the union was repealed (1922), when all Ireland save the six north-easterly counties in Ulster gained virtual independence. Those six, styled 'Northern Ireland', remained part of the United Kingdom, but with their own government and assembly (called Stormont, where it met) responsible for internal affairs. Stormont is the United Kingdom's single experiment of any duration in the devolution of legislative and executive power from London in the past century. Ill-fated from the start, it was finally terminated in 1972 in the face of terrorist and sectarian violence.

In modern times vibrant nationalist movements have persisted in Scotland, Wales and Northern Ireland, periodically assuming a potent political dimension within and without the established British parties. Nonetheless, federal concepts have found little favour in Britain – or, more accurately, in England, the union's 'predominant partner'. (See Table 1.1 – London alone has a population a quarter again as large as the whole of Scotland.) Devolved assemblies for Scotland and Wales, with legislative (though not tax-raising) powers, were almost established by Callaghan's Labour government in 1978/9; but the scheme foundered, and the United Kingdom's only subordinate executive tiers lie in a local government system whose discretionary authority has always been closely circumscribed by Whitehall and Westminster.

Table 1.1 The United Kingdom, 1987

	Electorate (million)	*MPs*
England	36.0 (83%)	523 (80%)
Scotland	4.0 (9%)	72 (11%)
Wales	2.2 (5%)	38 (6%)
Northern Ireland	1.1 (3%)	17 (3%)
United Kingdom	43.2	650

A sovereign parliament

'The sovereignty of Parliament', wrote the Victorian constitutionalist A. V. Dicey, 'is (from a legal point of view) the dominant characteristic of our political institutions': by which he meant 'neither more nor less than this, namely, that Parliament ... has, under the English constitution, the right to make or unmake any law whatever; and, further, that no person or body is recognised by the law of England as having a right to override or set aside the legislation of Parliament'.

Before analysing Dicey's classic exposition, it should first be noted that Dicey believed parliamentary sovereignty to be not merely a reality, but to be inevitable and essential, since 'limited sovereignty is, in the case of Parliamentary as of every other sovereign, a contradiction in terms'. In fact, few contemporary parliaments even formally possess such 'unlimited sovereignty': in most states, including all the former British dominions apart from New Zealand, they are limited either by federal divisions of the law-making power, and/or by constitutional enactments limiting their scope to pass laws violating fundamental freedoms, as typically set out in a Bill of Rights. Britain is virtually alone in being a unitary state which also has no Bill of Rights worth the name (the 1689 'Bill of Rights' simply guarantees Parliament's powers, it does not limit them).

The notion of parliamentary sovereignty both illuminates and obscures the actual power of Parliament. Illuminates, first, in three ways:

1. *Parliament does indeed possess unlimited legal authority to make any law or to amend any law already made.* Moreover, the scope for the courts to engage in *judicial review* – that is, to rule on the validity

of legislation and acts carried out under it − is limited to assessing whether or not powers exercised conform with the relevant statute. And if the judges find that they do not, Parliament can simply change the law − even retrospectively, if it so decides. By contrast, countries with written constitutions usually give the power of interpretation to judges, or a special tribunal, with power to override acts of the legislature if they are deemed to exceed limitations or conflict with rights stipulated in the constitution.

2. *Parliamentary supremacy is in practice accepted by Britain's major political and social groups*. This has not been invariably true, even of the recent past. The 1970s, in particular, witnessed a succession of organised challenges by major interest groups to the legitimacy of parliamentary legislation. In May 1974 the introduction of a devolved power-sharing executive for Ulster, supported by all the major parties in Britain, was sabotaged by a prolonged general strike in Belfast, backed by Protestant paramilitary organisations. On the mainland, bitter trade-union resistance to the industrial relations legislation of Edward Heath's Conservative government (1970−74) culminated in a miners' strike which virtually paralysed the country in the winter of 1973/4 and, indirectly at least, brought down the government. 'Who governs Britain?' was the Conservative slogan in the February 1974 election. It remained a live question for the rest of the decade, amid alarm that Parliament's authority had become no more than contingent on the goodwill of interest groups with muscle.

In retrospect, however, the alarm was exaggerated. The 1970s stand out as exceptional, and for more than ten years since the Thatcher government has had its writ obeyed implicitly. Even the Ulster Unionists and the miners have failed to challenge it successfully. Ian Paisley and James Molyneux's Ulster Unionists united to threaten disruption in an attempt to undermine the 1985 Anglo-Irish Agreement; but to no avail. The overtly political strike called by the National Union of Mineworkers in 1984 posed a more formidable challenge; but it was partial, poorly supported by the TUC, and Arthur Scargill had ultimately to concede defeat as the NUM's funds were sequestrated under the government's own union laws. Even that most bitterly contested of the Thatcher reforms, the poll tax (or community charge), has been implemented despite a vocal non-payment campaign promoted by the Scottish Nationalists and others.

3. *Parliament is supreme not only in legal and practical terms: it also possesses an undoubted political supremacy*. In Britain there is but one political arena, Westminster; all others are secondary and of little account. That is not to say that none but politicians matter in the decision-making process, still less that all − or even all important − decisions are made by MPs. On the contrary, as we shall see, Parliament can be little more than a side-show in the actual making of public policy. Yet the House of Commons remains the central focus of political life in Britain. It is in session for longer than any of its West European counterparts − for some 170 days a year usually extending to more than 1,500 hours in total.* Moreover, MPs *are* the political class in Britain; for uniquely among Western democracies, virtually all government ministers in Britain are first and foremost career parliamentary politicians. The rare exception (like Lord Young) simply proves the rule.

Parliamentary sovereignty thus has a legal basis, it is generally recognised, and it has a distinct political aspect. Nonetheless, the doctrine is inadequate as an explanation of the location of political authority in contemporary Britain, in four major respects.

1. *A legal fiction*. Parliament may be where sovereignty is formally exercised; it may even influence the decision-making process; but that does make it *the* supreme power in any meaningful sense. Ultimately, of course, the electorate is sovereign. Yet even that notion is simplistic, for the very means by which voters' opinions are aggregated and articulated − i.e. elections and parties − themselves serve to shape and distort them. The relationship between people, parties, pressure groups, power and Parliament is complex and multi-faceted, with each subject to a matrix of pressures and counter-pressures. It cannot be reduced to one neat doctrine about parliamentary supremacy.

2. *Self-restraint*. Perhaps the most potent prerogative of sovereignty is self-restraint, a sense of when *not* to act and what *not* to attempt. Dicey himself recognised this, for the 'sovereignty of Parliament' is only one of his two key constitutional doctrines: the other is 'the rule of law', a term intended partly to convey concepts such as 'legality' and 'government under law', but carrying with it assumptions as to

---

* By contrast, the West German Parliament (or *Bundestag*) meets for only about sixty-five days a year, while the French constitution imposes a maximum period for parliamentary sessions (not more than five and a half months a year).

judicial procedure and the exercise of power (like equality before the law and the avoidance of arbitrary discretion) which imply distinct limitations on 'sovereignty'. Moreover, politics is, in Lord Butler's dictum, 'the art of the possible'. The realm of the possible has no fixed boundaries: if nothing else, the Thatcher years demonstrate the capacity of a resolute government to break through even widely *perceived* limits. Nonetheless, constraints remain, in many respects (see below) greater than those pertaining in the past.

3. *Referendums*. In one important field – that of major constitutional innovation – Parliament has accepted the need for direct popular assent to change. British membership of the European Community (1973) and plans for devolution for Scotland and Wales (1978) were put to referendums after the necessary legislation had been passed – though, with the EC, also after it had taken effect. (The first produced a 2:1 vote in favour; the second yielded a 'no' vote in Wales and a narrow 'yes' vote in Scotland but with less than the 40% support of registered voters stipulated as necessary). A referendum would very likely be considered a prerequisite for major constitutional change in the future, parliamentary 'sovereignty' notwithstanding.

4. *External constraints*. 'No man is an island'; nor is any state in the developed world, even if it happens to be surrounded by sea with an imperial inheritance and isolationist tendencies. Britain is now more than ever before fettered by international obligations, the globalisation of economic activity, and the reality that many of the most critical problems facing government are not susceptible to purely national solution. Two institutions impose especial limitations on governmental autonomy:

   * *NATO*, an organisation of fourteen European states plus the USA and Canada, founded in 1949, is both a diplomatic alliance of the major Western powers and a defence organisation with integrated command, planning and operational structures. For more than forty years British defence and foreign policy has been intimately bound up with NATO and the 'special relationship' with the United States which largely depends upon it.

   * *The European Community (EC)* comprises twelve member states and more than 320 million inhabitants. It is the largest political and economic bloc in the world apart from China, and represents a bold and, of its kind, unprecedented experiment in confederal government.

Three aims lay behind the EC's foundation in 1957: the forging of a lasting European reconciliation with Germany, the progressive integration of member states' economies into a 'common market', and the creation of a political union, the nature of which was only partly defined. For these purposes the Treaty of Rome − the Community's founding charter − equipped the EC with its own decision- and rule-making body (the *Council of Ministers*), an executive board with an administrative corps (the *European Commission*), a consultative assembly (the *European Parliament*, which has been directly elected since 1979) and a tribunal to adjudicate on disputes concerning the founding treaties, the actions of Community institutions and rules subsequently enacted (the *European Court of Justice*).

It might be argued that Community membership, and the fulfilment of obligations arising from it, are no more than exercises of − not limitations on − the sovereignty of member states and their parliaments. Each freely chose to join; each can leave at will. Virtually all Community rules and decisions are made by ministers from member governments, all alike 'responsible' to national parliaments. In reality, however, the EC has become much more than the sum of its parts. Community officials and institutions wield powers involving frequent and substantial incursions into the national sphere, often to an extent unenvisaged when the powers were granted. The Community decision-making process, involving as it does continual bargaining between member governments at (often fraught and protracted) meetings of the Council of Ministers, can virtually oblige ministers to give British assent to Community acts without reference to Parliament − sometimes not even to the Cabinet.

The *Single European Act (SEA) 1986*, and the communal resolve of EC members to complete the single European market by the end of 1992, have further boosted the Community's authority. Despite the trumpets heralding the internal market, in the long term the Single European Act − an amendment to the Treaty of Rome signed by all member governments and enshrined in British law by Parliament − will probably prove the more important. For the SEA confers significant new powers on EC institutions; in particular, it gives the European Parliament a greater say in the making of Community legislation and enlarges the scope for the Council of Ministers to take decisions by qualified majority votes − i.e. without the consent of all member governments if necessary. Taken together with its preamble, which invokes the will of members 'to transform relations as a whole among their States into a European Union', the SEA represents a marked strengthening of the Community *vis-à-vis* its member governments and parliaments. Jacques Delors, President of the European Commission since 1985, has gone so far as to muse that 'in ten years' time 80 per cent of economic, and perhaps social and tax, legislation will be of Community origin'. Such remarks still arouse fierce antagonism, not least in the British Prime Minister. In her Bruges speech of September 1988, Mrs Thatcher invoked General de Gaulle's vision of a Europe of nation states (*Europe des patries*) and condemned any idea of 'a European superstate exercising a new dominance from Brussels'. Yet less than a year later, Commission plans for a comprehensive European Social Charter and a fully-fledged economic and monetary union were placed before the governments of the Twelve, with both likely to be implemented in some form. A 'superstate' may still be a remote prospect; but the growing power of Brussels has become a fact of British political life.

Government and Opposition

The pre-eminent function of the House of Commons is to sustain a government. Since general elections almost invariably yield a majority for a single party, sustaining a government and enacting its programme are primarily matters of party cohesion in the Commons. After each election, the Queen appoints the leader of the majority party as Prime Minister; he or she in turn appoints chief lieutenants to Cabinet posts and some seventy others to junior ministerial offices, who together constitute 'Her Majesty's Government'. The party's remaining MPs form the rank-and-file. Leadership and discipline thus issue from a party hierarchy in the Commons which *is* the government. Those MPs not members of the governing party form the Opposition. The largest non-government party is formally recognised as 'Her Majesty's Opposition'.

An essential precondition for the operation of the system of Government and Opposition is the existence of two parties commanding a majority of Commons seats between them. Two-party hegemony has been characteristic of British parliamentary politics since at least the Great Reform Act (see Table 1.2. for the last thirty years) and is often termed the *two-party system*. However, this term, ubiquitous though it is, must be treated with caution. If it purports to describe the *party* system, the implication that only two parties dominate British electoral politics does not correspond with the reality of recent electoral politics,

Table 1.2 Government majorities in the House of Commons, 1959–89

	Government MPs	Official Opposition MPs	Government majority	Party in Government
1959	365	258	101	Con
1964	317	303	4	Lab
1966	363	253	97	Lab
1970	330	287	31	Con
1974 (Feb.)	301	296	–	Lab
1974 (Oct.)	319	276	4	Lab
1979	339	268	44	Con
1983	397	209	144	Con
1987	375	229	100	Con

Note: Government majority over all other parties combined; the February 1974 election gave no party a majority, and Labour took office.

as will be seen in the next chapter. Yet if it is intended to refer to the *governmental* system, then the inference that the two parties broadly alternate in government must be qualified, since that has occurred only periodically over the past century. Indeed, one party (the Conservatives) has held power for fifty-eight of the last eighty-nine years, more than twice as long as its nearest rival (Labour); while of the twenty-four elections held since 1900, only ten have resulted in a change of government.

A cursory glance at the layout of the House of Commons chamber (shown in Figure 1.1) emphasises the dominance of Government and Opposition. MPs sit facing each other in rows, supporters of the government to the right of the Speaker (who chairs the House), opponents to his left. The ascendancy of the major party leaders is enhanced by their central location on the front benches of the two facing sets of rows, separated only by a table. Ministers sit on the front bench to the Speaker's right (sometimes called the *Treasury Bench*), Opposition leaders on the front bench to his left (hence the term *frontbench spokesmen*), whilst their respective 'unofficial' supporters sit on the benches ranged behind them (and are hence *backbenchers*). The Liberal Democrats and minor parties are relegated to benches on the Opposition

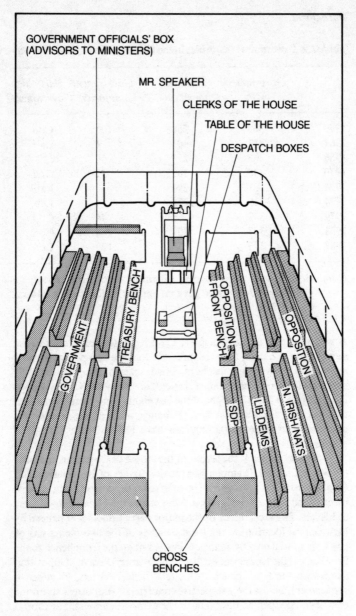

Fig. 1.1 The chamber of the House of Commons

side furthest away from the Speaker (*below the gangway*, as they are known). Two *despatch boxes* are situated on either side of the central table between the front benches, providing ministers and Opposition spokesmen with a commanding position from which to speak, and a waist-high box on which to rest their notes – no mean debating advantage!

Virtually all aspects of parliamentary life are dominated by the front benches. The Government takes most of the debating time available in both Houses for its own business; of the remainder, the Opposition has a special allocation of time to initiate debates of its own, while backbenchers have to make do with ill-attended Friday sittings and occasional slots elsewhere. The effective working of the parliamentary machine at every level depends upon frontbench co-operation. Mrs Thatcher gave a rare public acknowledgement of its importance in her welcome to Michael Foot as Leader of the Opposition in 1980:

May I warmly congratulate him on the assumption of his important office? I hope that he will genuinely and truly enjoy it. From time to time Prime Ministers and Leaders of the Opposition have to hold consultations. I know that those consultations will be pursued as amicably as they were with his distinguished predecessor (Mr Callaghan), to whom I am very grateful for all the cooperation we received during his time as Leader of the Opposition.

Such 'consultations' between leaders are infrequent; but the parliamentary managers of the two sides (called *whips*) meet continually to arrange business and related matters, a practice known as 'the usual channels'. Ultimately, the business of the House is directed by the Leader of the House of Commons, who is a Cabinet minister concerned above all to facilitate the passage of government business. Backbenchers play practically no part in the process.

The essential parliamentary functions of the Government are to initiate legislation in the public interest and in fulfilment of election commitments, and to justify its administration before both Houses – all activities which are examined in subsequent chapters. The parliamentary role of the Opposition is less straightforward, but almost equally important to the effective working of Parliament. It can be summarised under three headings:

1. *Expressive*. According to Bagehot the main role of the Commons, after installing and sustaining a government, is 'to express the mind of the English people'. The Opposition is vital to that expression.

In the first place, it is the political voice of a swathe of public opinion more or less excluded from the governing party's 'constituency' – with Labour in the 1980s, for example, the trade unions, the unemployed and the state-dependent. All parties help to fulfil this expressive function and a third party may – as with the SDP/Liberal Alliance in the 1980s – speak for a segment of opinion almost as great as the official Opposition, while the minor parties articulate voices – like the many in Northern Ireland – finding only a faint echo in Government or Opposition. But the Opposition's special parliamentary status makes it the chief instrument for the purpose, since its work in maintaining a close and continual criticism of the Government in Parliament – even when it is not actually opposed to ministerial measures – is a vital stimulant to the national political debate. As Sir Ivor Jennings put it:

Because the Government is criticised it has to meet criticism. Because it must in course of time defend itself in the constituencies it must persuade public opinion to move with it. The Opposition is at once the alternative to the Government and a focus for the discontent of the people. Its function is almost as important as that of the Government.

And as Jennings observed elsewhere, the reverse also holds: 'The purpose of parliamentary opposition is ... to appeal to the floating vote ... and to induce [the government] to modify its policy.'

2. *Alternative government*. The Opposition aims to replace the Government at the next general election. In the interim it conducts itself as a *shadow* government, complete with a 'shadow prime minister' in the *Leader of the Opposition, a Shadow Cabinet* (elected by Labour MPs, or appointed by the leader when the Tories are in opposition) and *Shadow Spokesmen* with portfolios broadly matching those of ministers, whose offices they aspire to take. In recognition of its role, the official Opposition receives most of the state funding (of about £1 million in 1989, known as 'Short money') available to opposition parties for office and research expenses.

3. *Parliamentary opposition*. 'The duty of the Opposition is to oppose, anything and everything.' The time-honoured dictum exaggerates the 'oppositional' role of the Opposition. Despite the clear ideological differences dividing the major parties, cleavages are much greater on general principles than on matters of practical policy. In the thirty-nine

parliamentary sessions between 1945 and 1983, 79% of government
legislation passed with its main principles unchallenged by the Opposition; indeed, surveys reveal a much greater tolerance of divergent
opinions and respect for qualities like compromise, co-operation and
flexibility among MPs than among the public as a whole. Moreover,
on some of the most significant policy areas, like Northern Ireland,
a broad consensus exists between the parties; while on others, like
Britain's relationship with the European Community, cleavages run
as much *within* as *between* the major parties. And, as we shall see, often
much the most effective opposition to a government comes from its
own backbenches, not from the benches opposite.

Nonetheless, the Opposition will, almost as a matter of course,
oppose the greater part of a government's programme with more or
less vehemence − even though it may not propose to reverse it all if
it wins office itself. Whatever the degree of cross-party consensus in
practice, the nature of Government and Opposition politics virtually
obliges both sides to adopt confrontational stands on most major issues.
The pros and cons of such an adversarial style of politics are much
debated; but if one of the Commons' main functions is to provide an
arena for the fighting of an ongoing election campaign, then it serves
that purpose. Ten years after Mrs Thatcher's first election, with Neil
Kinnock's 'new model' Labour party firmly established as the only
other serious contender for government, adversarial politics reigns
supreme − but it is clear that, if elected, the Opposition will accept
the bulk of its predecessor's legislation.

The decline of Parliament?

It has long been fashionable to deride Parliament as at best a talking
shop and at worst a rubber stamp, a diverting but essentially irrelevant
distraction from the 'real' business of politics and government.
For all the hot air expended in Parliament, so the argument runs,
decisions are taken not at Westminster but in Whitehall (or Brussels
or Washington) whilst the authentic political battle is waged well beyond
the ornate precincts of Lords and Commons. MPs no longer even
perform Bagehot's elective function. They simply register the verdict
of each election and entrust virtually unfettered power to the party
which emerges with a majority. On this view, the Thatcher years
witnessed the almost total eclipse of Parliament, as landslide majorities

and a presidential form of government made Lord Hailsham's 'elective dictatorship' a reality.

The following chapters are a commentary on that thesis. By way of preliminary remarks, however, two points need to be made. First, if Parliament has declined, it is unclear what it is supposed to have declined *from*. For at no time since Britain became a recognisable democracy has its legislature sought to assume the functions of government itself; equally, since then the essentials in the relationship between legislature and executive have remained unchanged. Secondly, it is facile to suggest that because Parliament yields up the work of governing to others, it therefore rests alongside the Crown in the dignified mausoleum of British institutions. Much confusion arises because, as Michael Ryle has observed, 'so many of the proceedings of the House [of Commons] are necessarily in a decision-taking form', with the government getting its way at almost every stage. Yet undue emphasis on the form masks the actual influence of the two Houses; it neglects the subtle but crucial role of Parliament, not only on the content of public policy, but in the shaping of political and govern-mental processes. The power of Parliament may be difficult to weigh and measure; but it is a reality nonetheless.

2
Elections and parties

Any British national aged at least twenty-one is free to stand for election to Parliament, provided that he or she is not a peer, lunatic, felon, bankrupt, civil servant, judge, clergyman of the churches of England or Rome − or a few other things besides. To do so they need only secure the signatures of ten electors and put down a deposit of £1,000, which is forfeit if they win with less than 5% of the votes cast.

There is, of course, far more to general elections than that. When are they held? How are candidates elected? What costs are involved? And given that membership of a political party is a prerequisite for success, what are the parties and how do they organise their affairs? This chapter addresses these questions, which between them determine not only the composition of the House of Commons but the framework of British politics as a whole.

The electoral cycle

Some democracies hold elections at fixed intervals, notably the United States, where elections for President take place every four years, for the House of Representatives every two, and for the Senate every six but with one-third of the seats coming up for election every second year. Others (like France and West Germany) hold elections at fixed intervals but with constitutional provision for an earlier poll in exceptional circumstances. In Britain, by contrast, there is no fixed interval between elections and no provision for a partial election. A general election is held whenever the Prime Minister of the day decides to call one, subject to three constraints:

1. *Five-year rule*. An election must be held at least once every five years (a stipulation of the Parliament Act, 1911). A majority of both Houses can vote to suspend this quinquennial rule, but since 1911 that has happened only in wartime (no elections took place between 1910 and 1918 or 1935 and 1945).

2. *Queen's consent*. The Queen has to issue a Royal Proclamation dissolving Parliament before an election can be held (polling day is usually three or four weeks afterwards, always on a Thursday). Her Majesty acts in this matter on the advice of the Prime Minister and no monarch this century has refused such 'advice'. But most constitutional lawyers believe that the Queen would be justified in refusing a request in exceptional circumstances − e.g. if a Prime Minister who had lost an election asked for another, despite the probable existence of a Commons majority for an alternative government.

3. *Commons majority*. Governments depend on the support of the House of Commons. If they fail to secure a majority on a formal motion of 'confidence' − or a vote of equivalent status − then the Prime Minister must either resign or call an election. Government defeats in such circumstances are, however, highly exceptional. Only two have occurred this century, and in both cases the party in government lacked an overall majority in the Commons − either because it had taken office without one (1924) or because a small majority had become a minority through the loss of *by-elections* (1979) (see p. 24).

It is often argued that prime-ministerial control over the timing of elections gives an unfair advantage to the party in power. In practice, though, the room for manoeuvre is limited and elections are held about once every four years − the last four being in October 1974, May 1979, June 1983 and June 1987. On only three occasions since 1945 has the interval between polls been notably shorter, and in each case an 'early' election was generally considered inevitable because of a government's small (1951 and 1966) or non-existent (October 1974) Commons majority. On the other hand, the argument often used to justify the existing system − that it allows elections to be called to resolve crises or to determine great national issues − is of dubious validity. Only one such election has been held since 1945: in February 1974 when Edward Heath called a snap poll in an effort to break a long and bitter miners' strike. But Mr Heath narrowly lost the election; and in so far as it resolved the strike, it did so in the opposite way to that which he intended. Indeed, most of the great post-war political 'shocks' – notably Suez, the Falklands and entry into the European Community – have been resolved without a special general election.

The electoral system

Politicians talk glibly of Parliament being 'chosen' by 'the people'. In fact, the only 'choice' each individual voter has is to fill in a ballot paper, which in Britain involves nothing more than placing an 'X' by the name of his or her favoured candidate. It is the system used for translating votes thus cast into parliamentary seats which determines who is elected – and different electoral systems can produce startlingly different parliaments from identical patterns of votes cast.

Most democracies use variants on one of two systems for translating votes cast into seats won:

* *proportional representation (PR)*, by which seats are allocated roughly in proportion to the distribution of votes between the competing parties across a country or region.

* *first-past-the-post* (or 'relative majority system'), by which a country is divided into constituencies of roughly equal size, each returning as its member the candidate gaining the largest single number of votes. (There is no 'post' as such: the phrase is one of the many racing metaphors that litter British political discourse.)

West Germany, Italy and Ireland are among democracies which use some form of PR; whilst Britain, the United States and most Commonwealth countries (notably Canada, New Zealand and India) use first-past-the-post.

The first-past-the-post system has three significant effects on the outcome of British elections:

1. *It exaggerates the lead of the winning party*. The United Kingdom is divided into 650 constituencies. To be elected, a candidate needs only to poll more votes than any of his rivals, even if he or she is thereby the choice of a minority of those voting. Here, for example, is the result of the contest for the Teesside constituency of South Stockton in the 1987 election:

Devlin, T. R. (Conservative)	20,833 (35.0%)
Wrigglesworth, I. W. (SDP)	20,059 (33.7%)
Scott, J. M. (Labour)	18,600 (31.3%)

The Conservative candidate was elected, although 65% of the electors did not support him. In practice, the party which gains most votes nationally usually accumulates them by taking first place in a majority of individual constituencies. Thus in all but two elections since 1945 the party polling most, but *less than 50%*, of the votes cast has won *more than 50%* of the seats in the House of Commons − by winning seats like South Stockton on a minority vote. In the 1987 election as a whole, Conservative candidates won 42% of the national vote but in the process took first place in 375 constituencies − giving the party 58% of the seats in the Commons (see Table 2.1).

Table 2.1   General election results, 1974−87

	1974 (Oct)		1979		1983		1987	
	%	Seats	%	Seats	%	Seats	%	Seats
Con	35.8	277	43.9	339	42.4	397	42.3	375
Lab	39.2	319	37.0	269	27.6	209	30.8	229
Lib/SDP	18.3	13	13.8	11	25.4	23	22.6	22
Nat	3.5	14	2.0	4	1.5	4	1.7	6
Northern Ireland parties	3.1	12	3.2	12	3.1	17	2.2	17
Total		635		635		650		650

This exaggerative quality is not a *necessary* feature of the first-past-the-post system. It is, rather, a consequence of one party's success, election by election, in gathering 40% or more of the vote spread so as to give it the highest average vote of the parties across most regions. In the last three elections the Conservatives have scored particularly in the densely-populated midlands and southern England, where they have secured an average of almost 50% of the vote. Furthermore, the Tories' lead over their nearest rival, Labour − 15% of the national vote in 1983, 12% in 1987, compared with a typical 5% separating the major parties in election between 1945 to 1974 − has secured them an even more disproportionately large share of seats than normal in the recent past. The post-1981 rise of the SDP/Liberal Alliance had much to do with this; but the relationship is not as simple as the comment 'the Alliance split the anti-Tory vote' might suggest.

2. *It under-represents third parties which lack a regional base*. A party will gain little or no representation in the Commons if its vote fails to rise above 35% or so nationally – unless it is concentrated efficiently so as to yield a large number of first places in individual constituencies. The bane of the Liberal party – in alliance with the SDP between 1981 and 1988 – was its perennial inability to achieve either target. Thus in 1987 the Liberal/SDP polled 23% of the national vote, but gained a mere 4% (twenty-two) of the seats in the Commons.

3. *It constitutes a high entry barrier to new parties*. The electoral system is thus a serious handicap to any new party. Since 1945, the only party (outside Northern Ireland) to have made even a modest breakthrough is the Scottish National Party (SNP), whose rapid rise north of the border in the late 1960s and early 1970s took it to a peak of 30% of the Scottish vote, and eleven of Scotland's seventy-one seats, in the October 1974 election. But the SNP was unable to sustain the challenge: it fell back to 17% in 1979, losing all but two of its MPs (though its prospects looked brighter again in the late 1980s).

Only two serious attempts at founding new national parties have been made since 1945, both in the 1980s:

* The *Social Democratic Party (SDP)* was launched in 1981 by four former Labour Cabinet ministers (Roy Jenkins, David Owen, Shirley Williams and Bill Rodgers), in response to the leftward lurch – as they saw it – of the Labour Party in opposition. At the outset the SDP proclaimed its intention to 'break the mould' of British politics and for a while it looked as if it might do so. Yet within seven years the SDP had succumbed to the electoral system. In alliance with the Liberals, it reached a peak of 25.4% of the vote in the 1983 election, the highest third-party vote in more than fifty years and only 2% short of Labour's tally. But that was still too little to yield the SDP more than a handful of seats and the party proved unable to push higher (in 1987 the Alliance fell back to 22.6%) – in no small part because of its inability, despite David Owen's dynamic leadership, to sustain momentum in the wake of the 1983 'defeat'. In its entire seven-year life as a serious political force, the party succeeded in electing only five new MPs, four of them in by-elections. The SDP did not break the mould; the mould crushed the SDP.

* The *Green Party* was founded as the Ecology Party in 1972, changing its name in 1985. Environmental issues came to the fore in British politics in the mid-1980s, but until 1989 the British Green Party

was so insignificant that to describe it even as marginal would be an exaggeration. In the 1987 election the Greens fielded only 133 candidates. They polled an average of 1.4% of the vote (the best performance was 3.6%), and not until June 1988 did the party feature in a national opinion poll. Its standing was transformed by the June 1989 European elections: on a surge of concern for all things Green coinciding with the disintegration of the centre parties, the Greens came virtually *deus ex machina* to take third place and 15% of the national vote – though, because of the electoral system, it won no seats.

The plight of third and fourth parties in Britain stands in stark contrast to the experience of their counterparts in European countries which use (or have used) some form of PR. In West Germany, Italy, France and Ireland new parties came from nowhere in the 1980s to take up to 10% of the vote and an equal share of parliamentary seats, and in one case (the Irish Progressive Democrats) even a junior role in government. The comparison with West Germany is particularly striking: the German Free Democrats (Liberals) have held the balance between the two larger German parties and played a key role in most post-war governments, with the support of around 8% of the vote in recent elections. The German Greens, who first entered the *Bundestag* in 1983 with a similar level of popular support, were considered possible coalition partners only six or seven years later. By contrast, Britain's SDP/Liberal Alliance, with three times the popular support of the German Greens or FDP, was a political neuter even in its heyday.

By-elections

When a Commons seat falls vacant – because the incumbent has died, resigned* or become a peer (i.e. a member of the House of Lords) – a *by-election* is held in the constituency to return a new Member. By-elections are critical to a government with only a small majority: James Callaghan's Labour government (1976–79) lost its overall Commons majority after defeat in several by-elections in 1976, and was forced into precarious dependence on the minor parties in order to stay in office. However, even when a government's majority is not in the balance, by-elections are still important for the extraordinary degree

---

* It is often written that an MP *cannot* resign. Whilst formally true, the process of 'applying for the Chiltern Hundreds', which disqualifies a Member from sitting and causes a by-election, is equivalent to an act of resignation.

of media and political attention they attract. They may only be glorified opinion polls, but they generate mid-term election fervour, in turn boosting and depressing the morale of the parties. Third parties are especially dependent on by-elections: all the post-war Nationalist and centre party surges have been stimulated by spectacular by-election successes, some of them – like Orpington in 1962, Hamilton in 1967 and Crosby in 1981 – sending tremors across the political landscape. For that reason the major parties avoid causing them wherever possible: between the 1983 and 1987 general elections only sixteen by-elections were held (Northern Ireland apart), eleven of them precipitated by the death of the sitting member.

Electoral reform

The effects of the first-past-the-post system have caused many to favour its replacement with some form of PR. But the debate on electoral reform is not, however, simply about 'fairness'. For general elections are legislative *and* executive elections, since the composition of the House of Commons determines which party shall govern – unlike, say, the United States where separate elections are held for the presidency and Congress, with the party controlling the White House often (as since 1980) in a minority on Capitol Hill. Arguments for and against reform thus relate both to the *quality of representation* and to the *effectiveness of government* provided by rival systems. The debate is further complicated by the fact that supporters of reform cannot agree on a replacement system. And whatever the alternative system posited, since Britain has never used any but the present, arguments on both sides involve continual hypothesising about the likely consequences of reform – with prognostications inevitably tailored to suit the respective protagonists.

A detailed survey of the pros and cons of electoral reform is beyond the scope of this book. But a grasp of the principal arguments involved gives a useful insight into the expectations held of parliamentary representation in Britain, and the extent to which they are believed to be realised.

Supporters of reform* rest their case on some of these arguments (among others) against the existing system:

---

* It is assumed below that reform would (a) involve the introduction of some markedly more propotional system of election; and (b) that such a system would typically result in no one party commanding an overall majority in the Commons.

1. It is undemocratic because it produces a House of Commons and government unrepresentative of electoral opinion.

2. It permits governments to wield untrammelled power, through a majority in the Commons, with the support of a minority of voters (as little as 39% in October 1974).

3. It fuels a damaging adversarial spirit in the political system, since parties have no need to co-operate in order to govern. Reform would engineer a more consensual style of government, affecting not only parties but the conflicting interest groups which support them.

4. It leads small shifts in electoral support for the parties to produce violent changes in the composition of the House of Commons, and thus to the policies pursued by governments.

5. It exacerbates an unhealthy 'north/south' divide in party representation. The cities of Glasgow, Liverpool, Manchester and Newcastle return not one Conservative MP between them; conversely, only three Labour MPs sit for seats south of a line from the Severn to the Wash, inner London apart.

6. It narrows the field from which candidates are drawn, discriminating in particular against women and ethnic minorities.

7. It makes it extremely difficult, in modern conditions, for anyone but the Conservatives to get into government. Labour supporters of PR further argue that the price of Labour's pursuit of office under the present system is a dilution of 'socialism' and a lurch towards the centre in an attempt to win the 'floating vote'.

Opponents of reform defend the first-past-the-post system on the following counts:

1. It gives every locality its own MP who takes up individual grievances and defends constituency interests at Westminster and beyond. Many of the proposed alternative systems would abolish the 'constituency MP'.

2. It may exaggerate the pattern of electoral support, but in practice the largest minority party, with the support of upwards of 40% of voters, almost invariably ends up in government. Under a reformed system such a party could be excluded by 'unholy alliances' producing governments and legislation *less* representative of opinion than at present.

3. It allows voters a clear choice of government. If coalitions became the norm in a reformed system, voters would simply elect a House of Commons; governments would then very likely emerge from lengthy and secretive horse-trading between parties after each election. Italy,

with forty-five post-war governments and regular political crises and parliamentary stalemates, is a favourite comparison.

4. Coalition governments – the inevitable consequence of a reformed system – would be inherently weak and unable to take 'tough' decisions. And if they took the form of small parties joining together with one of the major parties, then the minor parties would wield political clout out of all proportion to that justified by their electoral support.

Yet whatever the pros and cons of reform, the perceived self-interest of the two major parties (see Table 2.2), combined with the post-1987 collapse of the centre parties, look set to rule it out for some time – at least until one of the major parties, more likely Labour, changes its mind. It would, however, be misleading to attribute the survival of first-past-the-post to self-interest alone. Resistance to constitutional change runs deep in Britain, with no tradition of frequent switches of electoral system as elsewhere in Europe – all too often (France 1986, Greece 1989) unashamedly designed to benefit the party in power.

Table 2.2 Notional distribution of Commons seats by proportional representation, 1987 election

	% of total vote	Seats won	% of seats	Seats under PR
Con	42.3	375	57.7	275
Lab	30.8	229	35.2	200
Lib/SDP	22.6	22	3.4	147
Nat	1.7	6	0.9	11
Northern Ireland parties	2.2	17	2.6	14

The absence of reform in Britain is bound up with the nature of the parties winning and losing under the present system. Since the First World War the major loser has been the Liberal party – a centrist, impeccably constitutional force unprepared to challenge the legitimacy of electoral outcomes despite their manifest 'injustice'. Had an *extremist* 'anti-system' party succeeded in gaining around 25% of the vote but less than 4% of the seats in successive elections – or,

paradoxically, had such a party ever come close to winning an election
— then affairs might have been very different.

The cost of elections

The cost of fighting elections is another major 'external' constraint
faced by parties. In comparative terms, election spending by British
parties is modest, for two reasons:

1. *No TV or radio advertising*. Neither candidates nor parties are allowed to buy air time in Britain. Instead, in each election they are allotted
a set amount of TV and radio time without charge, called 'party political
broadcasts' (the major parties receive about five TV slots of ten minutes
each and similar time on radio). In countries which allow political
advertising on television, spending on TV commercials is the main call
on party and candidates' funds — and in the United States (empire
of the ad-man-cum-campaign manager) the sums spent on television
advertising are immense (a total of some $150 million — around £97
million — in the 1988 presidential election).

2. *Limits on candidates' spending*. Individual candidates are strictly
limited in the amount they can spend in election campaigns. The current
limit is about £5,000 per candidate per constituency. Personal wealth
is an undoubted advantage to a political career in Britain; but in no
party is it a prerequisite.

Nonetheless, there is no restriction on the spending of parties, locally
or nationally, *between* elections, nor on the spending of *national* parties
during elections, provided it is not on the broadcast media and does
not promote an individual candidature. The two major parties alone
spent some £25 million on the 1987 general election, and the exploi-
tation of new technology for elections — like the use of targeted direct
mail — is likely to increase spending still further in future. Moreover,
there is no state funding of political parties in Britain, in contrast to
other large democracies (France introduced it as recently as 1988), and
fundraising is a major preoccupation of the parties' national organisations. Finance has been a chronic problem for new political parties
lacking established corporate sources of funds: business in the case of
the Conservatives, the trade unions for Labour.

Parties

Political parties are largely unknown to the law. Until 1970 party labels were not even printed on ballot papers in general elections; and the party allegiances of MPs still do not feature in the official *Hansard* reports of parliamentary proceedings. Yet of the 650 MPs elected in 1987, all but one − the Speaker − belonged to a party and few, if any, besides him would have been elected without their party. In all, ten parties are represented in the Commons (in 1990); but four of them only contested constituencies in Northern Ireland and the vast majority of Commons seats − 605 out of 650 (93%) − went to the Labour and Conservative parties.

The party system and Parliament

In Britain party dominates Parliament, and Parliament no less truly dominates party. For almost all political parties in Britain are essentially *parliamentary* parties, in four respects:

1. Their primary object is to win seats in the House of Commons in order thereby to participate in − or at least to influence − government.

2. They accept the legitimacy of parliamentary government and urge obedience to laws passed by Parliament, although they may disagree with them.

3. They choose their leaders from among their MPs (groupings actually called *parliamentary parties*).

4. Their policies are to a greater or lesser extent determined by their MPs and parliamentary leaders.

More than 98% of votes cast on mainland Britain in the 1987 election went to parties conforming in all four respects.* Both major parties are led by MPs with long parliamentary experience − Mrs Thatcher had been an MP for sixteen years when elected party leader, Mr Kinnock for thirteen. Neither party questions the legitimacy of

* On the mainland only the Greens and the Nationalists dissent from them to any marked extent. The SNP's leader is not an MP and the party urged non-payment of the poll tax (though that could be considered as a ploy to boost its electoral support at Labour's expense); while the Greens deliberately eschew a traditional party structure − they voted against electing a single party leader at their 1989 conference. Northern Ireland is a case apart, but it is worth noting that of the province's two 'Catholic' parties, the constitutional Social Democratic and Labour Party (SDLP) polled nearly twice as many votes in 1987 as the pro-IRA Sinn Féin (21.1% to 11.4%).

Parliament, though sections of the Labour party − mainly outside Parliament − have been equivocal. The precise status of MPs may differ between the parties, but in both they play a pre-eminent role and − in practice if not always in theory − take the lead in the formulation and exposition of party policy.

Party leaders

Though the leaders of the major parties must be MPs, they are chosen in different ways:

 * *Conservative* leaders are elected by Tory MPs alone. They are now subject to re-election at the start of each parliamentary session, but there have only ever been two serious contests − in 1965 when Edward Heath succeeded Sir Alec Douglas-Home, and in 1975 when Margaret Thatcher challenged and − after an acrimonious contest − defeated Mr Heath. As Heath found to his cost, Conservative leaders are secure only until they lose an election.

 * *Labour* leaders used also to be elected by their party's MPs alone. But a new system was agreed by the 1981 Wembley conference by which the selection of leader and deputy leader − both of whom must be MPs − is made by an electoral college in which 40% of the votes are cast by affiliated trade unions, 30% by constituency Labour parties and 30% by Labour MPs. Only one leader − Neil Kinnock in 1983 − has been elected by the college, and both he and his deputy (Roy Hattersley) won majorities in all of its three sections.

 * The *Liberal Democrats* and *SDP* elect their leaders in a postal ballot of all paid-up party members. Paddy Ashdown was elected the Liberal Democrats' first leader in 1988; David Owen has never been contested for the SDP leadership.

Once elected, leaders have wide discretion in their selection of party spokesmen from among their parties' MPs. *Conservative* leaders are unfettered in their choice, in or out of office, and the Tory leader also appoints the Chairman of the Conservative Party who supervises the party's organisation and public relations. *Labour* leaders are more constrained: when the party is in opposition, its eighteen-strong 'Shadow Cabinet' is elected by the party's MPs, though the leader allocates portfolios among those elected and can appoint additional spokesmen. When in office, a Labour Prime Minister is initially bound by the rules of the Parliamentary Labour Party (PLP) to include in his Cabinet those elected in the last Shadow Cabinet election; but thereafter no such restriction applies. Whatever the formal position, however, leaders have only a comparatively small pool from which to draw; and the necessity of maintaining a balance between the different 'wings' of the respective parties among their leaderships imposes its own constraints – though more so for Labour than Conservative leaders, as some ministers learnt to their cost in Mrs Thatcher's successive reshuffles.

Selection of parliamentary candidates

The selection of parliamentary candidates is, arguably, the most important function carried out by the organisations of the major parties. For in at least 500 of Britain's 650 constituencies one or other of the parties is, in choosing a candidate, effectively selecting the next MP. In the 1987 election only forty-six seats (7%) changed hands between parties, and in only a further 151 (23%) was the winning majority 10% or less – the point beyond which a seat is generally considered invulnerable to an ordinary election swing.

In deciding who shall be MPs, the *electorate* is therefore of far less importance than the *selectorate* – that is, those in the major parties with responsibility for selecting parliamentary candidates. The electorate as a whole plays no part in this process – in contrast to the United States, where 'primary elections' give electors a vote in the selection of their party's candidates for the election proper (whether it be for the presidency, Congress or state offices).

The nature of the British selectorate varies between parties:

* *Conservative* candidates are chosen by a selection committee appointed by each constituency executive. Before they can be chosen by a local party they have first to become an 'approved candidate', which involves interviews by MPs and party officials at Conservative Central Office in London. There are only about 500 approved candidates.

* *Labour* also has an 'approved list' while leaving the actual choice to local parties. Until recently, the general management committee of each local association made the selection; but there have been moves to allow ordinary party and union members to have a greater say. At present, general management committees shortlist applicants, but the selection from among them is conducted through an electoral college, with 40% of the votes cast by affiliated trade unions and 60% by individual members of the constituency party.

* The *Liberal Democrats* and *SDP* also have central lists of

approved candidates. Each constituency executive draws up a short-list and a candidate is then selected through a ballot of party members, at or after a hustings meeting.

It is from this selection process that Members of Parliament emerge, and it is with them that the next chapter is concerned.

3
Members of Parliament

The history, structure and essential features governing the election and workings of the House of Commons were outlined in Chapters 1 and 2. So far, though, the Commons has been a set without a cast. This chapter introduces the *dramatis personae*: the 650 men and women elected to serve as Members of Parliament. What sort of people are they and what do they do in and out of Westminster? How do they see their role and how has it changed in recent years? And what resources do they have to carry out their functions?

Today's MPs

'I have always thought', wrote the Victorian novelist Anthony Trollope, 'that to sit in the British parliament should be the highest object and ambition of every educated Englishman.' In Trollope's time, the House of Commons was indeed filled with 'educated Englishmen'. The typical Victorian MP had been to a public school (likely as not Eton), to college at Oxford or Cambridge, and was either a lawyer or a scion of the landed aristocracy; above all, he was a thoroughbred gentleman and proud of it. His typical 1990s successor also went to public school (though not Eton), to university (with an evens chance of it being Oxbridge) and is either a professional or – as a businessman with accumulated wealth – a latter-day 'gentleman of independent means'. He will hail from no great family: on the contrary, he will probably be a 'self-made man' and proud of it. But he will still be every inch an Englishman, with equal emphasis on the 'English' and the 'man'; and by education and occupation he will be no less *au fait* in the circles that matter in contemporary Britain.

Table 3.1 surveys the occupational background of MPs elected in

Table 3.1 Occupations of MPs elected in 1987

Occupation	Con	Lab	SLD/SDP	Other	All (%)
Barrister/solicitor	64	18	6	2	14
Doctor/dentist	3	2	1	–	1
Architect/surveyor	7	–	–	–	1
Engineer	6	–	–	1	1
Accountant	17	2	–	1	3
Civil servant/local gt	13	8	1	–	3
Armed services	15	–	1	1	3
Lecturer/teacher	28	57	4	9	15
Scientific research	3	6	–	–	1
Total professional	156	93	13	14	42
Company executive	114	9	–	1	20
Commerce/insurance	18	1	–	–	4
Management/clerical	4	9	2	2	4
Other business	3	1	–	–	1
Total business	139	20	2	3	28
Misc. white collar	8	18	2	–	4
Political activist	21	12	1	1	5
Journalist/publisher	26	14	3	–	7
Farmer	16	2	1	1	3
Other misc.	7	4	–	4	2
Total misc.	78	50	7	6	22
Miner	1	16	–	–	3
Skilled manual	2	44	–	1	7
Semi-/unskilled	–	6	–	–	1
Total manual	3	66	0	1	11
Grand total	376	229	22	23	

Source: Based on D. Butler and D. Kavanagh, *The British General Election of 1987* (Macmillan, 1988), pp. 202–5.

1987. The Tories, unsurprisingly, have most of the businessmen in the Commons whilst Labour's ranks include a large minority of manual workers. That said, the major difference between the parties' MPs lies not in class-distinctions but in the *type* of middle-class professional they recruit: a quarter of all Tory MPs are private-sector professionals (mainly lawyers and accountants) whilst 40% of Labour's contingent come from the public-sector professions (mainly teaching and lecturing). In all, more than four-fifths of MPs have professional, executive or managerial backgrounds, compared with less than one-third of the working population at large.

However, occupation gives only half the picture. In terms of age, education, sex and race, MPs are no more socially representative. More than two-thirds are aged between forty and sixty. Nearly half were educated at public schools (68% of Tories) and two-thirds went to university — some 32% to Oxford or Cambridge alone (see Table 3.2).

Table 3.2 Education of Labour and Conservative MPs elected in 1987

	Labour		Conservative	
	No.	*%*	*No.*	*%*
School				
Eton	2	1	43	11
All public schools	32	14	256	68
State secondary school	197	86	120	32
University				
Oxford & Cambridge	34	15	166	44
Other	95	41	97	26
All universities	129	56	263	70

Source: As Table 3.1

A mere 6% are women. Ethnic minorities, who now make up nearly 5% of Britain's population, saw only four of their number returned to the House of Commons in 1987 (with Keith Vaz the first Asian MP for sixty years). Like any assemblage of 650, 608 of them men, the Commons finds room for eccentrics, social misfits, even downright crooks. Two Conservative MPs retired at the 1987 election due to disclosures that they had made multiple applications for privatisation share issues; a flamboyant MP went amid newspaper allegations involving 'rent-boys'; and a Labour MP stood down after a conviction for indecency. Others involved in *causes célèbres* were re-selected by their parties and re-elected by their constituents.

MPs are thus a select breed. The old aristocratic 'governing class' has long since passed away; but in its own way today's ruling corps is not much less élitist. Why is the Commons so exclusive, and should it be a matter of concern? After all, Parliament is supposed to represent the people as a whole. How can it do so when its composition is such a poor reflection of British society?

These questions go to the heart of the nature and purpose of representation in a democracy. To address them in practical terms, three distinct issues must be addressed: the institutional rigidities within the system for choosing MPs; the characteristics of political life which in effect restrict it to a small number; and, finally, a more value-laden issue, the qualifications necessary for the job of representative: how important is it for an MP to 'represent by reflection', or are other qualities equally or more desirable?

1. *Institutional rigidities*. The British electoral and selectoral systems severely narrow the field from which MPs are chosen. By and large, the selectorate, itself a predominantly middle-class cohort, discriminates against men without a professional, political or managerial background and – at least until recently – against women of all kinds. And before candidates even reach the constituency selectorate, they face a weeding-out process by the national party. All prospective Conservative candidates, for example, have first to go though a two-day national selection exercise, and only about half are successful in getting on to the national list. In a rare lifting of the veil, Tom Arnold, the Conservative Party vice-chairman responsible for candidate selection, spelled out the qualities sought in Tory candidates:

Are they leaders? Could they weld a Conservative association together, lead it into an election campaign, and, if successful, represent the constituency in the House of Commons. Are they well-rounded individuals who can cope with the stresses and strains of public life, domestic pressures, and constant travelling?

The Conservative Party is not looking for experts, but it is looking for men and women who have a good working knowledge of contemporary politics and a proven track record of experience in the party, and who above all know their own minds.

Moreover, the single-member constituency system exacerbates prejudice against women and ethnic minority candidates since it obliges each local party association to choose its *single* most favoured candidate from a shortlist. Proportional systems of election, involving the selection of candidates in *groups* chosen partly with an eye to maximising the party's electoral appeal, tend to yield a larger number of women candidates. In the Scandinavian countries, all of which have PR systems, a quarter to a third of MPs are women; this can be partly accounted for by the region's political and cultural development, but its electoral system is a contributory factor. In West Germany, where a mixed party list and single-member constituency system is used for elections to the *Bundestag*, the great majority of women deputies are elected through the lists (sixty-three of the seventy-seven women elected in 1987, including more than two-thirds of the women deputies representing the two major parties – though the latter between them win most of the constituency seats which make up 60% of the *Bundestag*).

The House of Commons is, however, more socially representative than virtually all its Western counterparts in one important respect: it possesses a comparatively high proportion of manual workers. In all, 12% of MPs elected in 1987 had a 'manual worker' background, including sixteen former miners. They owe their election to the Labour party's selection procedures. Labour maintains a central list of union-sponsored candidates and this, together with the bias of some constituency parties – particularly those dominated by a powerful trade union with a substantial local membership – in favour of candidates with 'working-class' credentials, gives trade union activists a special opening. Even so, 'workers' are in a minority even among the half of Labour MPs who are union-sponsored, and their number is declining.

2. *Political life.* Whatever selectoral and electoral rigidities apply, at least four characteristics of British political life limit it to a tiny group in any case:

    * *Small political class*: few people have much interest in politics and far fewer are politically active. Barely 2% of the electorate so much as belong to a party; and only a fraction of those have the single-minded ambition and dedication almost invariably essential to becoming an MP.

    * *Time*: politics is time-consuming, and often prohibitively so at the level necessary to gain and sustain a parliamentary nomination.

For example, more than a third of the major parties' MPs were formerly local councillors, and a similar proportion fought at least one unsuccessful parliamentary contest before winning a seat. Most parliamentary candidates never win a seat. MPs inevitably tend, therefore, to come from those occupations most compatible with parliamentary ambitions.

  * *Education and political skills*: the qualities normally requisite for political advancement, particularly in a brief encounter with a selection committee – ambition, social ease, administrative competence, public speaking ability – are more characteristic of the so-called 'articulate professions' (law, teaching, lecturing) than of other occupations.

  * *Politics as a career*: once elected, most MPs regard the Commons as a career and give it up only involuntarily. The turnover of MPs is thus low, and the duration of parliamentary careers long. The typical Member has been in the House for upwards of fifteen years (more than 100 MPs had served for longer than twenty years in 1989); eighty-seven MPs retired at the 1987 election, the highest number to stand down at any election since the war, but that was still less than one-seventh of the Commons. Moreover, in Britain the great majority of political careers start young and – in contrast to other Western countries – there is little movement in or out of Parliament at late career stage. Unless a budding politician is in the Commons by his mid-to-late thirties, his chances of ascending the ministerial ladder are slim. (Mrs Thatcher was elected at the age of 34, Neil Kinnock at 28, John Major at 36 and Roy Hattersley at 32.)

Most future MPs are socialised into politics early, if not through a political family then at university or through a trade union. Student politicians, in particular, take themselves almost comically seriously: the executives of campus unions, the National Union of Students and the Oxford and Cambridge Unions, are crammed with would-be MPs, not a few of whom reach the Commons without ever doing a 'real' job. (Mrs Thatcher was president of Oxford University Conservative Association in 1946; Neil Kinnock president of the student union at University College, Cardiff in 1966.)

3. *Desirable qualifications*. There is no job specification for the post of MP. Even so, two points should be made about the post. First, even were it desirable, it is practically impossible for an MP to 'represent by reflection' given the heterogeneous social make-up of Britain's localities. Secondly, an MP's role is not akin to that of, say, a juror

or lay magistrate, requiring only a modicum of common sense, a readiness to perform civic duty and a sense of what is and is not 'acceptable' to the community as a whole. An MP ought, of course, to be accessible to his constituents and attuned and responsive to their sentiments. But the House of Commons has, corporately, to be able to undertake the multifarious activities surveyed in this book — government, opposition, law-making, scrutiny, public debate and the rest — and its prime resource for the purpose lies in its members. To paraphrase Bagehot on Sir Robert Peel, what the Commons needs is not geniuses, but men and women of common opinions and uncommon abilities.

Women in the Commons

It is now more than seventy years since women gained admission to the Commons — or *re*admission, perhaps, since abbesses sat in the Saxon *Witenagemot* some ten centuries ago. Before 1914 the Suffragettes' passionate struggle for equal political rights for women was met with arguments that female MPs would trivialise debate, jeopardise the well-being of their families, even that they would require escorts home after late-night sittings. Some years after Nancy Astor had taken her seat in the Commons, the first woman to do so, Winston Churchill told her: 'When you came into the House, I felt as though a woman had entered my bathroom and I had nothing to protect me except my sponge.'

Since 1919, however, women have been notable in the Commons not for their triviality so much as for their startling absence. For in the past seventy years only 141 women have been elected to the Commons. In the 1987 election forty-one women were returned, the largest number of female MPs ever (and among them the first ever black women Member, Diane Abbott); but they represented barely one-fifteenth of the House. At the ministerial level women have fared still worse: since 1919 only forty women (twenty-two Labour, eighteen Conservative) have held government office; a mere eight of them at Cabinet level.

Sex discrimination has played some part in keeping women out of Parliament. Local parties have traditionally been hesitant to choose women candidates, particularly for 'winnable' seats. This was still the case in 1987 (Table 3.3): only 14% of candidates were women, and their success rate was less than half that of men — one in eight women candidates was elected, compared to one in three men.

Table 3.3   Women candidates and MPs in the 1987 election

Party	Cands	Women	%	MPs	Women	%	Success rate (%)	
							Men	Women
Con	633	46	7	375	17	5	61	37
Lab	633	92	15	229	21	9	38	23
Lib	327	45	14	17	1	6	6	2
SDP	306	60	20	5	1	20	2	2
Other	426	84	20	24	1	4	7	1
Total	2325	327	14	650	41	6	31	13

Yet, discrimination is only part of the story. The fact is that until recently few women have wanted to stand for Parliament in the first place – proportionately far fewer than pursue other traditionally 'male' professions or take part in local government. In terms of female representation, Britain is not far out of line with other Western democracies which use the 'first-past-the-post' system – indeed, the Commons contains more than twice as many women as both Houses of the United States Congress put together.

However, things are changing. The number of women MPs more than doubled in the 1980s, with a record number (327) of female candidates in 1987 and no fewer than seven women ministers in the government two years later. This may, in part, be the result of recruitment efforts by the parties. In 1980 the all-party '300 Group' was formed to campaign for a minimum of 300 women MPs. By 1990 it had not succeeded in persuading any of the parties to follow the practice now increasingly common in the rest of Europe – particularly in Scandinavia – of imposing formal or informal quotas, but the selection procedures used by Labour and the centre parties now provide for at least one woman to be on each shortlist of candidates. The Conservatives have not followed suit (which may account for their paucity of women candidates); but it was, of course, a Tory woman who first achieved the supreme office and who held it continuously for longer than any of her male predecessors in more than a century and a half.

What impact have women made on the Commons? It is often said that Parliament devotes more time to women's and children's issues than it used to. In so far as they can be distinguished, that is undoubtedly true, but it is not clear that their increased prominence has much to do with women MPs. Certainly, *private member's bills* (see Chapter 5) successfully introduced by women have tended to involve 'feminist' issues; but arguably the most important such bills affecting women in the last twenty years – David Steel's 1967 Abortion Act and three subsequent attempts to reform it, most recently by David Alton in 1988 – were all sponsored by men. In any case, most legislation derives from the government, and it is hard to relate ministerial concern for female- and child-related issues to the lobbying of women MPs independently of wider social pressures and changes in attitude which have made themselves felt in recent decades.

The House of Commons thus remains a male bastion. Its few women members complain periodically of a rigidly masculine atmosphere, and comparisons with a boys' public school still abound (an analogy which some men appear quite happy to endorse – see p. 90.). Parliamentary hours make normal family life an impossibility – even if there were childcare facilities in the Palace of Westminster. Symbolically, seventy years after Lady Astor first took her seat, the Commons has a barber but no women's hairdresser. It would be rash to predict how long it will be before one is *in situ*.

MPs and parties

For centuries past, politicians and constitutional lawyers have grappled with the fundamental issue of whether the MP is essentially a *representative* who should act according to his own judgement, or a *delegate* who should do the bidding of his constituents and/or party; and, if the latter, from whom he should take instructions.

Edmund Burke was not the first or last to condemn any idea of the MP as delegate, but he put it best in his address to his Bristol electors in 1774:

[An MP's] unbiased opinion, his mature judgement, his enlightened conscience, he ought not to sacrifice to you, to any man or to any set of men living ... Your representative owes you, not his industry only, but his judgement; and he betrays, instead of serving you, if he sacrifices it to your opinion ... Parliament is not a *congress* of ambassadors from different and hostile interests ... but ... a *deliberative* assembly of *one* nation, with *one* interest, that of the whole.

In terms of contemporary party politics, however, the distinctions between 'industry', 'judgement' and 'opinion' are at best blurred, at worst meaningless. For an MP does not represent only his *constituency*; he also represents his *party*. Parties may, to a greater or lesser extent, share common beliefs and ideals; but the very essence of party politics in a liberal democracy lies in each party having its own view of the '*one* interest' of the '*one* nation'. And unless an MP is at least broadly in sympathy with that 'opinion', he would not have been selected to exercise his 'judgement' in the first place.

This does not make an MP a mere cipher. On the contrary, in the major parties, policy is largely the creation of the parliamentary leadership, reflecting opinion in the parliamentary party as a whole. To paraphrase Burke, MPs have ample opportunity to see to it that party opinion is sacrificed to *their* judgement. And the higher an MP rises in his party, the greater his scope for doing so – though even ordinary backbenchers have ample opportunities, through the media, party forums and Commons devices like *early day motions,** for drawing attention to, and organising support for, their views. Nonetheless, from time to time ruptures do occur between MPs and their national or local parties and the issue of party discipline has been a live and at times controversial one in the past twenty years.

MPs and local parties. The great majority of MPs enjoy cordial relations with their local parties, rarely (if ever) meeting hostile attempts either to mandate or to 'deselect' them (i.e. to withdraw the party nomination). But even if relations become fraught, the options open to a local party are limited. It cannot formally mandate an MP and, if it did, anything purporting to be a mandate would have no legal standing. Nor can an association force its MP to resign before a general election is held. Its only recourse is to seek to deselect the MP, but this is no mean task in either of the major parties. A Conservative Member

---

* An *early day motion (EDM)* is a motion tabled 'for an early day' and printed on the Commons' daily order paper. EDMs are never debated, but they provide an opportunity for backbenchers to make political points and to show the degree of support for them – within or across parties; they can also be useful for highlighting a constituency interest. The last few years have seen a dramatic rise in the number of EDMs: in the 1959/60 session only 111 were tabled; by 1985/6 the number had reached a record 1,262 – an average of 7.4 per sitting day. This escalation has caused some concern, particularly at the extent to which MPs are simply tabling EDMs drafted for them by lobbyists; but the Procedure Committee (3rd report, 1986/7) noted that 'the tabling of EDMs does act as an outlet for the opinions and emotions of backbench Members' and came out against any restrictions.

can only be deselected by a vote at a general meeting of all members of his constituency association, and in the recent past only one has been so dismissed for his political views – Sir Anthony Meyer, MP for Clwyd NW, in January 1990. (Meyer had, however, just stood against Mrs Thatcher for the party leadership, the authentic act of a kamikaze.) It is easier to deselect a Labour MP, since party rules oblige all MPs to undergo a reselection – in which rival candidates can stand – during the course of each Parliament. When 'mandatory reselection' was first introduced in 1981 there were fears that it would precipitate bitter conflict between 'moderate' Labour MPs and 'extremist' local parties. There have indeed been such conflicts – the most celebrated being the deselection of Frank Field, a widely respected and independent-minded Labour MP, by his Birkenhead constituency party in December 1989. But the number of deselections has been comparatively small – only seven in the 1983–87 Parliament, with barely a quarter of the 177 Labour MPs standing for reselection even subjected to a ballot. As Denis Healey puts it: 'A Member of Parliament who works hard in his constituency and is trusted as a human being by the active members of his local party can normally count on personal loyalty to override differences about policy.'

MPs and national parties. The main source of discipline facing an MP comes not from his local but his national party. For Labour MPs this can mean the party conference, which has policy-making powers and can, *in extremis* (as, for example, in 1981 over unilateral nuclear disarmament), endorse policies repugnant to a majority of Labour MPs. There is no equivalent body in the Conservative Party: the Conservative Party Conference is hardly more than a rally, with no policy-making powers. One former Tory leader said he would rather take advice from his valet than from a Tory Conference. In any case, the 'national party' generally means the leadership of the parliamentary party, which maintains discipline through managers called *whips*. The word has its origins in the hunting age ('whippers-in' kept the hounds on the scent), and in practice it now has two connotations:

  * *Party Whips.* The leaders of the two major parties appoint a dozen or so whips; in both cases they are headed by a *Chief Whip*, also appointed by the party leader (except for Labour in Opposition, when the Chief Whip is elected by all Labour MPs). The Chief Whip – depending on whether the party is in or out of office – is a member of the Shadow Cabinet or *de facto* member of the Cabinet. One of the

main tasks of the whips is to ensure that backbenchers support party policy in Commons votes. Stories of the tyranny of whips abound; Harold Wilson went so far as to say, during a period of backbench discontent in the late-1960s, that 'every dog is allowed one bite, but a different view is taken of a dog that goes on biting all the time ... He may not get his licence renewed when it falls due'. But the whips' day-to-day role is not primarily concerned with cajoling the racalcitrant. On the contrary, the whips' major role is to act as the party leader's eyes and ears in the parliamentary party – continually channelling back-bencher's views upwards and keeping a genial watch on the activities and concerns of the MPs in their charge. The whips also play a key role in organising Commons business, on the floor and in committees.

* *The Whip* is the formal notice of forthcoming Commons business sent by the Chief Whip to all his party's MPs weekly during the session. Votes involving matters of party policy are delineated by an underlining of the relevant business three times – hence a *three-line whip*. MPs are expected to be present and vote with their party on all three-line whips; in certain circumstances they can 'pair' with an MP from the other side (if they have one to pair with), but if they feel unable to support their party – which happens only rarely – then they may have to explain themselves to their Chief Whip. Persistent dissidence will wreck an MP's chances of promotion to ministerial office and can, exceptionally, lead to sanctions, the ultimate one being withdrawal of the whip (i.e. expulsion from the parliamentary party). Less important votes are denoted by *one-* and *two-line whips*. A *free vote* is a division on which no formal party 'line' applies, when MPs are officially free to vote as they see fit; they are mostly confined to moral issues like abortion and capital punishment.

The whipping system is not as draconian as it might appear. For it is a product as much as a cause of the high degree of cohesion within Britain's parliamentary parties. Party leaderships, themselves drawn from, and more or less representative of, their MPs as a whole, are usually sensitive to backbench sentiment in laying down party policy. As for the whips themselves, their job is, in Paul Silk's words, more that of personnel manager than disciplinarian. Moreover, the system is not inviolate. MPs can and do defy the whips, and they have been doing so with increased frequency in recent decades. Since Edward Heath's government of 1970–74 backbench rebellions, sometimes on a dramatic scale, have been a fact of everyday parliamentary life, though governments rarely actually suffer defeats in the Commons.

Party and Parliament are thus inextricably intertwined in Britain, but it is a mistake to see the second as no more than a pawn in the hands of the first.

The role of the Member of Parliament

Since no such creature as the 'average MP' exists, generalisations about 'the role of the MP' can be trite and misleading. There is the world of difference between, say, a Cabinet minister sitting for a marginal seat who devotes almost every hour of every day to ministerial, party or constituency business, and an Opposition backbencher with a large majority, a practice at the Bar and no ministerial ambitions, for whom politics is a part-time pursuit. Nevertheless, dissimilarities of *lifestyle*, however great, should not be confused with differences of *function*. For MPs share broadly similar functions, which can be summarised under five headings.

1. *Party loyalist.* The pre-eminent role of MPs collectively is to sustain a government in office. The House of Commons does not create governments as such: that is done formally by the Queen and in practice by the Prime Minister she appoints (see p. 12). But immediately after its formation, every government must submit a programme to the Commons in the form of the Queen's Speech; and if a majority votes against the Speech, or subsequently carries a motion of no confidence (or a resolution tantamount to one), the Prime Minister must either resign or call an election. In theory, therefore, each individual MP – or, more precisely, 326 (a majority) of them acting in concert – wields power of life and death over a government. In reality, MPs invariably vote with their party leaders on motions of confidence and governments fall only if their party lacks a Commons majority. No government has fallen through the adverse votes of its own MPs for more than a century.

This needs to be emphasised because it is now fashionable to dwell on the increasingly independent proclivities of MPs. In the past twenty years Members have indeed shown a readiness unprecedented in post-war years to vote against their party whips, even on matters of importance. This has not been without consequence, as we shall see. But the confines of such overt dissension are limited; and when it does occur it is, in Richard Rose's words, 'usually a lone wolf phenomenon'. In particular, it remains highly exceptional for government back-benchers to defy the ministerial whip in sufficient numbers to inflict a defeat, and so ingrained is party loyalty that a hostile vote is normally given only in the secure knowledge that it will *not* put the government in a minority. Moreover, concentration on formal rebellions ignores the more informal − but no less significant − aspects of the relationship between frontbenchers and backbenchers. As Peter Riddell has put it, 'the continuing process of give-and-take between ministers and backbenchers' is a normal part of parliamentary life, and 'this behind-the-scenes process reflects the simple, but often overlooked, point that ministers are MPs and spend much of their time, including most evenings when the House is sitting, with friends, colleagues and rivals who are backbenchers'.

Thus for all the sniping by groups of Conservative MPs − notably dismissed ministers and the remnants of the 'wets' − against Mrs Thatcher's government, it has only *once* been defeated in the Commons on an issue of significance in its decade of office − in April 1986 when the Sunday Trading Bill was rejected by MPs − and even that was a peculiar case (see p. 67). And it should not be thought that the present government is a case apart because of its landslide majorities. Even the 1974−79 Labour government, which had a bare or non-existent majority and faced repeated attacks from a group of chronically mutinous 'left-wing' backbenchers, lost only 1.5% (23 out of 1,505) of the Commons votes it faced through defections by its own MPs, and not one of those defeats was of sufficient gravity to bring it down. MPs may now increasingly be prepared to play the 'lone wolf'; but even for the few habitual wolves party loyalty is the norm, and absolutely so on occasions when their vote could affect their party's chances of remaining or becoming the government.

Exacting though the dictates of party loyalty may be on an MP's conscience, they are far from time- or effort-consuming to meet. Indeed, an MP's duties as party loyalist hardly extend beyond voting as directed by the party whips and periodically reporting back to his constituency party executive − a largely nominal imposition for Tories, though rather more serious for Labour MPs. It is in other roles that MPs find most of their occupation and fulfilment.

2. *Party activist*. Most MPs are partisans as much by conviction as necessity and devote their time largely to party activity − whether in the Commons, their constituencies or through pressure groups and the media (where self-promotion goes hand-in-hand with advancing the cause).

At Westminster, party activity has its formal and informal sides. Every Labour MP is a member of the *Parliamentary Labour Party (PLP)*, which meets weekly for at least an hour during the session, and has a committee structure embracing some nineteen subject and nine regional groups. Most Labour MPs also belong to one or more of the party's parliamentary factions – the most prominent being the 'soft-left' Tribune Group and the 'hard-left' Campaign Group, both of which run 'slates' of candidates for elections to the Shadow Cabinet when the party is out of office and have extra-parliamentary organisations concerned to influence party policy and personnel. Conservative MPs are less factionalised. All backbench Tories belong to the *1922 Committee* (so named after the year of its foundation), which elects officers and, like the PLP, has a plethora of subject and regional committees. As for Tory caucuses, there are numerous informal groups, some of them – like the Monday Club, the Tory Reform Group, and the '92 Group' of dedicated Thatcherites – with a pronounced ideological edge; but a minority of Tory MPs belong to them and in practice, apart from periodic agitation for and against candidates for posts in the 1922 committee elections, they are little more than talking shops.

Until the rise of the mass media, most political campaigning took place in the constituencies, led by MPs and opposing candidates. Nowadays, constituency activity is limited: MPs seek publicity in local press, radio and TV, and may support or lead campaigns with their local councillors and other 'grass roots' activists – particularly in the run-up to an election. Beyond that, the political battle is fought in London in TV and radio studios and (to a lesser extent) in the national press. A sizeable number of MPs make some contribution: former Cabinet ministers like Tony Benn and Michael Heseltine resolutely refuse to fade from the public eye, while backbenchers like Austin Mitchell, Ken Livingstone and Edwina Currie seem rarely to leave the major broadcasting studios and are better known than not a few secretaries of state. For the most part, however, it is party leaders and their principal lieutenants who engross the media's attention. Almost anything said or done by the Prime Minister and Leader of the Opposition is newsworthy, while on a day-by-day basis, policy statements, political 'happenings' and run-of-the-mill events automatically attract interviews from ministers and their Opposition counterparts.

It is important, in this context, to stress the overwhelmingly

Westminster-centred nature of Britain's political media. Virtually all 'domestic' political news is created in and reported from Parliament – the very titles of political journalists ('lobby correspondent', 'Westminster editor', etc.) bespeak the assumption. Senior politicians who lose their seats in the Commons find it virtually impossible to stay in the limelight, try as they may, as Shirley Williams and Enoch Powell, to take recent electoral casualties, have found to their cost.

3. *Constituency representative*. MPs declare incessantly that their first duty is to their constituents. What do they mean?

From time immemorial one of Parliament's principal functions has been to address grievances brought before it; and as the scope of government has expanded enormously since the war, so have the grievances. 'Thirty years ago', as Lord (Jim) Prior puts it in his memoirs, 'an MP would have to look for work and go and search for the problems in his constituency. Today the burden of constituency surgeries and the many cases which come to an MP's attention through his post are enormous.' The 'burden' takes four broad forms:

* *welfare work*: MPs typically receive upwards of 100 letters a week and most hold regular advice 'surgeries' in their constituencies. Many MPs also maintain a constituency office, often with a secretary specifically to deal with local 'casework'. Letters and surgeries are for the most part taken up with individuals' grievances, opinions and requests for information. There is almost nothing on which an MP may not be approached, but health and welfare issues predominate (see Figure 3.1). MPs deal with their casework largely by correspondence with the relevant government departments (ministers receive about 9,000 letters a month from MPs when parliament is sitting), local authorities, local DSS offices, and so on; but they also have recourse to oral or written parliamentary questions of ministers, and exceptionally they may raise a constituent's grievance on the floor of the House in an adjournment debate. As a very last resort, they can refer cases of alleged maladministration by a public body to a statutory investigator known as the Ombudsman (see p. 104).

MPs thus spend much of their time being glorified social workers. But most of them protest that welfare work is a vital part of their job. Denis Healey argues this forcefully in his memoirs:

Every MP should act as a Miss Lonelyhearts. The busier a politician is with national or international affairs, the more important is his constituency case work. It is that above all which keeps him in touch with the problems of those

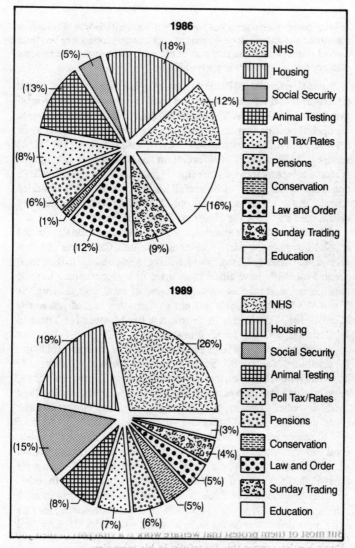

Fig. 3.1 MPs' postbags and constituency surgeries, 1986 and 1989
MPs' responses to the question: *Which of these subjects do you receive
most letters about in your postbag or receive most approaches about
from individuals in clinics or other ways?*

he is supposed to represent, and teaches him how legislation at Westminster actually affects real people on the ground − or how powerless it is to help them ... And this is perhaps the only part of his work where he may see concrete evidence that his existence is worthwhile.

* *public relations*: MPs act as a point of contact between national government and administration and local councils, pressure groups, businesses and charities. The benefit is reciprocal. Local bodies value the special hearing they receive and the openings MPs provide, while MPs value first-hand contact with local organisations. A 1989 MORI survey of MPs' sources of information found that 69% highlighted 'visits to company factories/premises' (generally within the Member's constituency) as their 'most useful' source, while 37% mentioned 'constituents' − compared with only 20% who noted parliamentary committees and 26% the House of Commons library.

* *local notable*: MPs and their spouses are leading local figures and expected to play the part − opening buildings, fêtes, school prize-givings, and other good works which bring them publicity in their local press. Most MPs have either their main or a second home in their constituency and take on an active round of local engagements. As Truro MP Matthew Taylor has put it: 'here they regard you as the Member for Westminster in Truro; not the Member for Truro in Westminster, and you forget it at your peril'.

* *local promotion*: a large proportion of MPs are active lobbyists for constituency social, cultural and economic interests. A recent study by D. M. Wood, based on interviews with seventy Conservative MPs, revealed that more than half regarded their work in pursuing localised industrial policy strategies, and lobbying ministers and others to further them, as a 'normal and important part of their role'.

The same study also found, tellingly, that MPs' enthusiasm for such local entrepreneurial activity correlated not with a constituency's level of social deprivation but with the size of the MP's majority: the safer the seat, the less likely is a Member to lobby, and that goes for the other activities described above. Even so, constituency activity makes no more than a marginal difference to an MP's re-election prospects: his fate is far more dependent on the regional swing to or from his party than the hours he spends as 'Miss Lonelyhearts'. Popular and hard-working Members usually build up a small personal vote, and in each election a few incumbents survive because of it. But truly dramatic survivals against the trend are to be found only among the small number of third-party MPs, and most of those − like Rosie Barnes, Simon Hughes and David Alton — owe their seats to victory in peculiar and highly publicised by-elections in the first place. Such durability is exceptional even for third parties: of the twenty-two Labour MPs who defected to the SDP in 1981 and defended their seats in 1983, only three were still MPs after the 1987 election — and of those three, David Owen probably owed his re-election more to his national than local standing.

Finally, it must be emphasised that certain services are *not* provided by MPs. Lobby as he may, an MP has no hoard of government jobs or grants to dole out to supporters and constituents. The agents of Whitehall and County Hall alone dispense state-funded largesse, and the strict party régime in Parliament leaves no room for individual MPs to roll the pork-barrel in the style of their American counterparts (though governments, acting on behalf of a majority of MPs, are not above temptation). Moreover, MPs who are not ministers have no formal standing in the administrative structure. Their headed letter paper produces swift replies, but no special favours. In the work of government, as Ivor Crewe puts it, 'the MP is not a player but a spectator, albeit with a front-stall seat'.

4. *Member of the Commons.* Two popular misconceptions about the work of MPs hold the field: that they make the law, and that they spend most of their time making and listening to speeches in the House of Commons. In fact, as we shall see, most law is practically made by the time it reaches Parliament; the role of MPs collectively extends little beyond conferring legitimacy upon legislation drawn up elsewhere. So far as debates are concerned, the House does not even meet until 2.30 p.m.,* and an MP typically spends little more than an hour a day in the chamber — long enough for *Question Time*, especially *Prime Minister's Question Time* on Tuesdays and Thursdays and perhaps for the opening speeches of a major debate. Later in the evening (usually at 7 p.m. and/or 10 p.m.), MPs may briefly assemble in the chamber again for a vote, but only occasionally will more than a handful have sat through the debate on which they are voting. As for speaking, the average backbencher can only expect to be called in major debates three or four times a year.

The allure of the TV cameras may make the chamber rather less deserted a battleground; but whether in the chamber or not, MPs

* Except on Fridays, when business starts at 9.30 a.m. — but Fridays are *private members' days* and rarely do more than a few dozen MPs turn up.

nonetheless still spend the best part of each day at Westminster when the Commons is sitting. Committees, correspondence and party and constituency business between them occupy most of the time of backbenchers, while ministers and Opposition spokesmen also have departmental affairs to attend to. But it is not all work. The Commons, its lobbies and corridors, its bars and terraces, its dining room and smoking room, its gossip and ambience, *are* the political world in Britain. 'When I am ill I am in bed; when I am not I am in the House of Commons', Sir William Harcourt once remarked; and that remains as true now as when said a century ago. Even the busiest minister has an office in the Commons and keeps part of most days free to be in 'the House'. Decision-making may largely take place in Whitehall; but the decision-makers spend longer at Westminster than in Downing Street.

It used to be said that the British MP, like the British civil servant, was an amateur all-rounder. That remains true in some senses. The comparative weakness of the Commons' committee structure, the strictures of party discipline and the persistence of a 'generalist mentality', all stand in the way of Members developing anything like the thoroughgoing specialisms of their US Congressional counterparts; and, as we shall see, the facilities at MPs' disposal give a veneer of amateurism to their efforts. There is not even a proper induction course for newcomers. Little has changed in that respect since Tony Benn noted in his diary, shortly after the 1966 election:

I gave my first tea party for the new [Labour] MPs. About fifty turned up and they were touchingly grateful. The fact is that the Party has done nothing to greet them ... They gathered round and asked me a lot of questions from 'How do you get a pair?' to 'How do you put down a parliamentary question?'

Even so, most MPs have or develop a keen interest in some area of policy – whether from personal, constituency, ministerial or other motives. The departmental select committees, in operation since 1979, give about 150 backbenchers an opportunity to specialise and to make political capital out of their specialism. Their importance in this regard should not be overstated: many Members are attracted to select committees because of *existing* specialisms, and at least as many as sit on them acquire specialist interests and knowledge from ministerial or frontbench offices. Select committees operate within a narrow sphere, with nothing approaching the status or resources of their Congressional counterparts. In the words of one senior backbencher,

MPs' specialisms are more akin to a 'continuing interest that will rise and subside according to pressures and counter pressures' than to genuine expertise. The 'House of Commons man' is still an all-rounder at heart; but for the most part he is a far more articulate and hard-working one than his predecessor of even twenty years ago — so much so that he can sometimes come to look beguilingly like a real expert.

5. *Ministerial aspirant*. It was said above that MPs have no standing in the administrative structure *qua* MPs. At any one time, however, about one-sixth of the House of Commons, appointed from the majority party, direct the administration as ministers. For by convention, all but a dozen or so members of the government must be in the Commons, making (in November 1989) 20 cabinet, 51 junior ministerial and 11 whips' posts available to MPs, in addition to some 40 *parliamentary private secretaryships*.* In all, therefore, about a third of the governing party's MPs hold government posts — and are known collectively as the 'payroll vote'. The size of the 'payroll' is such that, given the rate of electoral and ministerial turnover, most Tory and Labour MPs with a degree of nous and circumspection, and able to hold their seats, believe themselves to have a fair chance of holding office. Statistically, they are right: the number making it to the cabinet is small (only some forty MPs are present or past cabinet ministers); but a quarter of the entire Commons are past or present ministers or whips.

Each MP builds up an individual role from these five functions, though one which may change sharply — perhaps more than once — over the course of his parliamentary career. By any objective standard the first of the five functions outlined — that of party loyalist — is the most consistently important. But, perhaps unsurprisingly, a survey by Donald Searing of more than half the Commons in the mid-1970s found MPs themselves divided in their self-assessments. Forty per cent

* A *parliamentary private secretary (PPS)* is an unpaid political assistant to a minister. The duties of the post are undefined, but most PPSs act as aids to their ministers in the Commons and also serve as two-way channels of communication between them and backbenchers. Though not formally part of the government, PPSs are generally bound by the convention of collective responsibility to support the government in the Commons; and since the post is often the first step on the ministerial ladder, most PPSs are happy to accept the restraint. According to Philip Norton, almost half (9 out of 19) of cabinet ministers and three-quarters of junior ministers (46 out of 63) in place in January 1989 were former PPSs.

believed their primary role lay in 'supporting and criticising the executive'; of the rest, 25% believed it lay in constituency service, whilst 25% put ministerial aspirations at the top of the list. Whatever their role, almost all MPs are alike in leading hectic and stressful lives in which, to take John Patten's entry in *Who's Who*, 'talking to my wife' is relegated to a 'hobby'. As a recent study by Radice, Vallance and Wallace concludes:

MPs currently work over 60 hours a week and collectively keep the longest and latest hours of any Western Parliament; they seldom have a free weekend, and see little of their families. When the House is sitting, many backbenchers are on one or two Committees a week, attend daily Question Time in addition to numerous meetings ... and those with far-flung constituencies travel endlessly. Deluged by letters from constituents, their postbags also bulging with pressure-group circulars, they struggle towards their weekend constituency surgeries where local cases add to their burden. And if not all members are quite so overworked as this suggests, the description probably fits most of them some of the time and some of them all of the time.

For all that, few MPs willingly contemplate a career outside politics. Even after retirement, a fair number of them – more than 150 at present – cling to Westminster by accepting peerages and entering the Upper House. With Lords (Harold) Wilson, (James) Callaghan and (Roy) Jenkins facing Lords (Alec Douglas-) Home, (William) Whitelaw and Hailsham, dozens of their former colleagues in tow, the House of Lords of 1990 makes a jaded but recognisable impression of the House of Commons a quarter of a century ago – the epitome of 'life after death', as Jeremy Thorpe once quipped.

MPs' pay, allowances and facilities

MPs were paid for the first time in 1911. Since then, MPs have collectively determined their own remuneration, though subject to strong government pressure. The salary level was an ongoing matter of dispute between the two until 1988, when the Commons voted to peg MPs' salary to a fixed point on the civil service salary scale, equivalent to that of an assistant secretary at grade six. In 1990 this was equivalent to £26,701 a year, a substantial increase – in real as well as nominal terms – on the £6,897 payable in 1979. Even so, a recent report estimated that more than two-thirds of MPs have outside earnings or occupations of some kind,* and some backbenchers — and even some ministers, who earn far more — claim not to be able to 'manage' on their official stipend alone. By way of comparison, in 1989 US Congressmen were paid $89,000 (around £57,000), set to rise to $125,000 (around £80,000) by 1991.

MPs receive numerous allowances in addition to their salary. They can claim expenses up to a set limit for travel on parliamentary business and travel warrants for spouses, secretaries and children under the age of eighteen for journeys around the triangle of home, constituency and London. In 1988 a total of almost £5 million — an average of some £7,600 per member — was paid for travel. Further allowances include pension provision for Members' staff, a London supplement for those with constituencies in inner London and an overnight allowance for those whose homes are further away.

By way of facilities, MPs receive free stationery, telephone and postal services at Westminster, strictly for use on parliamentary business (but noone checks). They are also paid an allowance to cover secretarial and research assistance — £22,588 in 1989, a dramatic increase on the £4,200 of 1979 (secured through backbench rebellions against the government in 1983 and 1986) and sufficient to employ one full-time and one part-time secretary and/or research assistant at the going rate. The increased costs allowance is reflected in the number of staff employed by Members — up from 816 in 1982 (1.4 per MP) to 1,344 by March 1988 (2.1 per MP). Some MPs also have unpaid research help (at any one time a hundred or so — mainly US — interns give their services for a pittance). Research facilities are also provided by the Commons Library, whose establishment has risen from thirty-two in 1960 to more than 150 in 1989 to cope with increased demands from MPs.

Despite substantial improvements in the 1980s, facilities available to MPs still leave much to be desired. Fewer than 200 Members have an office of their own; the rest share at least one between two, with barely enough room for two desks and chairs apiece. A new building for MPs and their staffs is currently under construction at Bridge Street (opposite the Palace of Westminster and around the corner from the

* No restriction is placed on MPs' outside earnings, but since 1975 the House has imposed a requirement on its Members to register certain financial interests, including financial sponsorships, paid directorships and employment, and substantial interests in land and shares. The register is publicly available.

Norman Shaw buildings, the latter converted to parliamentary office space in the mid-1970s). When Bridge Street is completed in the early 1990s, every MP will have an office of his own — and British MPs will at last enjoy the basic amenities long taken for granted by other Western parliamentarians.

Yet when all is said and done, few MPs are in the job for the money.

> Fame is the spur that the clear spirit doth raise
> (that last infirmity of noble mind)
> To scorn delights, and live laborious days.

And for all the laborious days, parliamentary life is not devoid of delights. In particular, the Palace of Westminster's bars and restaurants are numerous, lavish and heavily subsidised. The overhead and payroll costs of parliamentary catering are paid directly by the Treasury. Despite that, the Commons refreshment department managed to notch up an estimated net loss of nearly £2.5 million in 1988/9. Part of the deficit was incurred through the construction of a grand new pavilion on the Commons terrace, overlooking the Thames. Doubtless the pavilion, which serves excellent (and evidently under-priced) Pimm's, provides some solace from the strains of elected office; at any rate, it helps to keep Parliament the best club in London.

4
The Speaker and officers of the House of Commons

'With the exception of the Sovereign herself', it has been written, 'there is probably no holder of high public office whose prestige exceeds that of the Speaker'. For the Speaker is not merely chairman of the House of Commons; with the Monarch, he symbolises the continuity and authority of parliamentary government itself. And ever since Speaker Thomas opened radio broadcasting of the Commons in 1978 with his rich Welsh rendition of 'Order! Order!', the Speaker has been a household voice, if not name. This chapter describes and assesses the role of the Speaker and the other officers and staff concerned with the management of the Commons.

The Speaker

History

The office of Speaker dates back to the earliest days of the House of Commons in the late fourteenth century. Originally an agent of the King, the Speaker increasingly came to be considered an officer of the Commons, a guarantor of its rights, and those of minorities within it, against the oppressions of monarchs and ministers. 'I have neither eyes to see, nor tongue to speak in this place', as Speaker Lenthall told Charles I when the King entered the Commons to arrest five Members in 1641, 'but as the House is pleased to direct me, whose servant I am here.' In fact, it was not until the unrivalled thirty-three-year speakership of Richard Onslow in the mid-eighteenth century that the Speaker came to be seen as an impartial 'servant' of the House; and it was another century before Speakers were invariably above the political fray. In the recent past, however, the Speaker has never been an active partisan like his namesake in the US House of Representatives (who effectively leads the majority party), or the presiding officers of other European parliaments.

Until the late nineteenth century the Speaker's duties extended little beyond presiding over sittings of the House. It was the rise of serious obstruction of Commons proceedings in the 1880s, led by Parnell's Irish Nationalists, at a time when governments were increasingly seeking to enact substantial programmes of legislation year on year, which led to a transformation in the Speaker's standing. Over the next thirty years he was given wide-ranging powers to regulate and curb debate, and broad discretion in their exercise. By the First World War the essentials of the modern Speakership were firmly established.

Election

The Speaker is elected by the House of Commons from among its Members. Once chosen, he immediately resigns from his party. But he continues as an MP while in office, and if he wishes to remain Speaker for more than one Parliament stands in his constituency as 'Mr Speaker seeking re-election'. No modern Speaker has been defeated at the polls: indeed, a few have been re-elected without opponents from the major parties. The Speaker continues to fulfil constituency duties while in office, though he cannot use the floor or committees of the House to air grievances.

'Members should feel', Churchill once declared, 'that the election of Speaker arises, as it were, from the whole body of opinion in the House.' It is conventional, however, for the Speaker to come from the party in office at the time of a vacancy. The Prime Minister takes the initiative in the selection, though none is made until after informal consultation with backbenchers and other parties in the House. By the time the Commons meets to elect a Speaker, the choice is generally agreed and only rarely contested on the floor of the House.

The current Speaker, Mr Bernard Weatherill, has been in post since 1983. He was previously Deputy Speaker and before that Deputy Conservative Chief Whip. The Deputy Speaker often succeeds as Speaker, but there is no convention to the effect: both of Speaker Weatherill's predecessors (Selwyn Lloyd and George Thomas) were former Cabinet ministers. By contrast, Weatherill's roots are firmly in the backbenches, and it is widely believed that his selection owed much to backbench resistance – from all parties – to the election of the former Tory Cabinet minister favoured by Mrs Thatcher.

Functions
The Speaker has four principal functions:

1. *Chairman of the Commons*. The Speaker chairs sittings of the House of Commons. In that capacity all speeches and remarks are addressed to him and he calls speakers to address the House. With 650 members belonging to ten parties, all vying for the opportunity to ask questions and put their points of view, it is no easy task to ensure a fair balance and protect the rights of backbenchers and the smaller parties. But the Speaker's job is made easier by reliance on precedent, by conventions regarding the ordering of speakers (e.g. ministers followed by Opposition spokesmen in debates) and by rules limiting the duration of backbench speakers to ten minutes in debates in which pressure to speak is great. Beyond that, the Speaker has absolute discretion in the selection of Members, though some Speakers have kept records of those they have called, particularly at Prime Minister's Question Time, to help them ensure fairness and impartiality.

The Speaker has a range of discretionary powers at his disposal, all conferred by the House itself. He can select motions and amendments for debate; he can accept or refuse to put motions to curtail debate; and he can permit private notice questions to be tabled or emergency debates to be held. He also adjudicates in first instance over complaints of breaches of privilege (allegations that someone has committed a contempt of the House). In exercising these powers, the Speaker is guided by convention and past practice where relevant.

The Speaker has three deputies who chair the House in his absence and possess his full powers when so doing. He (or his deputy) only votes if there is a tie when, by convention, a casting vote is given in favour of the status quo. To ensure that neither side is disadvantaged by one of its members taking the Chair, the Deputy Speaker (who by convention does not vote either) is invariably chosen from the opposite party to the Speaker; the other two deputy Speakers are usually chosen one from either side.

2. *Regulation of proceedings of the House*. It is the Speaker's duty to ensure that the rules of the House are observed. These rules are laid down in Standing Orders, past resolutions, and Erskine May's *Parliamentary Practice*, a treatise on parliamentary procedure running to over 1,200 pages and regularly updated by the *Clerk of the House*. The Speaker may rule on points of order or procedure in the course

of debate; he can also discipline individual MPs for breaches of order, his ultimate sanction being to 'name' an offending MP, which usually results in the Member's suspension from the House (normally for a period of five sitting days for the first 'offence', twenty for the next, and indefinitely thereafter). In cases of general disorder, the Speaker can suspend a sitting on his own authority; but even when tempers flare, the Speaker's authority is such that he can usually restore order.

3. *Ceremonial*. The Speaker's traditional duty of conveying formal messages from the Monarch to the Commons now has little practical or ceremonial application. But there remains a large ceremonial element in the Speaker's role. He wears court dress (complete with wig and robe) when in the Chair, moving in stately procession before each sitting from his residence in the Palace of Westminster (the 'Speaker's House') to the Commons chamber. He also takes part in a regular succession of ceremonial duties at home and abroad in his role as chief representative of the Commons in its corporate relations with the Lords, the Monarch, outside institutions and foreign parliaments.

4. *Administration of the Commons*. The Speaker is *ex officio* Chairman of the *House of Commons Commission*, a statutory body of MPs, set up in 1978, which employs all the permanent staff of the House and directs its five departments (see Table 4.1). Matters relating to accommodation, services and facilities for MPs are dealt with by the select committee on House of Commons Services.

Table 4.1   House of Commons administrative staff

	No. in 1979	No. in 1988
Clerks	58	61
Dept of the Clerk of the House	61	89
Speaker's Office	10	11
Dept of the Serjeant-at-Arms	181	186
Dept of the Library	118	156
Dept of the Official Report	70	84
	498	587

The Speaker has other incidental functions, some of them occasion-ally significant, like his role as president of conferences on electoral reform, set up periodically to consider changes to the electoral laws. Taking his duties together, it will be clear that two qualities are necessary in a Speaker. First, strength of character and an air of command. Second, a strict impartiality in all public matters and a position above party political controversy. In Laundy's words, 'Once in the Chair he becomes in the truest sense a House of Commons man', and im-mediately on retirement he leaves the Commons and accepts a peerage. Recent Speakers have been criticised on both counts: Speaker Weatherill for his lax control of the House and Speaker Thomas for his somewhat censorious memoirs. But the prestige of the office remains untarnished.

The Leader of the House of Commons

In contrast to the Speaker, the Leader of the House of Commons is a party politician and Cabinet minister appointed by the Prime Minister. Until the First World War the Prime Minister, when an MP, acted as Leader himself. No post-1918 Prime Minister has done so, but the post is usually held by a senior member of the Cabinet, who is sometimes dubbed the 'Deputy Prime Minister' (as with R. A. Butler in the 1950s, Michael Foot in the 1970s and the current incumbent, Sir Geoffrey Howe).

'Manager' would be a more appropriate title than 'Leader', since the Leader does not actually lead. That role still belongs to the Prime Minister, who is the government's principal spokesman and leads for it in the most important debates. The Leader's role, rather, is to ensure the efficient running of the Commons and, with the Government Chief Whip, the smooth passage of government business. Both roles require a consensual persona: an effective Leader must be able to co-operate with his Opposition 'shadow' on business matters and needs to be sensitive to the grievances and concerns of backbenchers of all parties, even if (as is the norm) he is prepared to do little about them.

The Clerk of the House and other Officers

The Clerk of the House is the senior official of the House of Commons, who keeps its official journal and acts as principal adviser to the Speaker, the Leader, and MPs generally on matters of practice and procedure. On appointment, the Clerk will typically have spent virtually his entire career in the Clerk's department and will have an almost unrivalled experience and knowledge of the work of the House. The Clerk also has responsibility for managing his own department, which comprises some sixty clerks along with about 100 other administrative staff – all recruited through the Civil Service selection process, though by status they are employees of the Commons, not civil servants. In addition, the Clerk is a member of the House of Commons Commission, with an influence on the management of the Commons extending far beyond his own department.

Besides the Clerk, a number of other officials are responsible for Commons administration. Of the more important, the *Serjeant at Arms* acts as 'Master of Ceremonies' in the Commons and is responsible for security and domestic matters. (*Black Rod* performs the equivalent role in the Lords, including the annually televised ritual of marching from the Lords to summon MPs to hear the Queen's Speech and having the door slammed in his face.) The *Department of the Official Report* is responsible for the production of *Hansard*, the authorised verbatim record of the proceedings of both Houses which for more than a century has been published and circulated the day after each sitting. The *Librarian* is responsible for the Commons Library and with it for a department of more than 150 staff, including a substantial research division which provides a research and information service for MPs. Two other officials – the Ombudsman and the Comptroller and Auditor-General – perform important functions relating to the scrutiny work of the Commons, and their role is considered in later chapters.

The Commons employs more than 500 administrative staff in all (see Table 4.1) – a marked, but far from dramatic, increase on the position ten years ago. If the officials of the House of Lords are included, the total still comes to fewer than 700, making Parliament one of the most sparsely staffed of Western legislatures. The United States Congress, to take the other extreme, employs more than 20,000 administrative staff either directly or in support agencies specifically to service Congressmen. In terms of research and administrative resources, Westminster is the poor relation of modern parliaments.

5
The legislative process

The *Oxford English Dictionary* defines a legislature as 'a body of persons invested with the power of making the laws of a country or state'. In fact, as we have seen, Parliament is not the *only* 'body of persons' with power to make the laws for the United Kingdom; and its role in 'making' laws in any case usually largely consists in confirming measures drawn up by the government. Nevertheless, most laws applicable in Britain require the consent of Parliament, and the giving of that consent is a lengthy and complicated business.

For a law to be made (or 'enacted'), a *bill* (or draft statute) must be laid before one of the two Houses of Parliament. To become law, it has then to pass through an elaborate procedure of scrutiny in both Commons and Lords, at the end of which both Houses must agree on an identical text (though if the Lords fails to agree with the Commons, there is provision for MPs to override the peers). When this has been achieved, the Queen signs the bill and it thereby becomes an *Act of Parliament*. The whole procedure is known as 'the legislative process'.

This chapter is concerned with the principal types of bill and the legislative process to enact them.

Types of bill

There are two main types of bill: *public bills* and *private bills*. The distinction between the two lies in the intent behind them: a public bill must relate to a matter of public – i.e. general – interest and be introduced by an MP or peer; whereas a private bill is a proposal to change the law to benefit a particular person, group of people or corporate body, and is introduced by the prospective beneficiary. Public bills are much the more important of the two since all government legislation is enacted by means of them. The description below of the legislative process is that applicable to them. Private legislation will be considered at the end of this chapter, along with secondary legislation.

One further distinction needs to be made. In practice (though not formally), public bills are divided into two categories: government bills and private members' bills:

* *Government bills.* A government bill is simply a bill promoted by a minister. It may be anything from a highly controversial measure implementing a key aspect of the governing party's election manifesto to a minor measure intended simply to bring together, without changing, the law in a given field. The government's major legislative projects of each year are announced in the Queen's Speech which inaugurates the session, and thereafter consideration of government bills is the single most time-consuming activity of both Houses. To give some idea of their scope and significance, these are the more important government bills promoted in the 1988/9 session alone:

Bill	Purpose
Bill	*Purpose*
Water	To privatise and restructure the water industry
Electricity	To privatise and restructure the electricity supply industry
Football Spectators	To set up a compulsory national membership scheme for Football League clubs
Dock Work	To abolish the Dock Work Scheme
Children	To reform the law governing the care and protection of children
Official Secrets	To prohibit disclosure of official information 'harmful to the public interest'
Prevention of Terrorism	To provide anti-terrorist measures
Local Government	To reform parts of the local government system
Companies	To reform parts of company law
Social Security	To impose stricter requirements on claimants of state benefits

* *Private members' bills (PMBs)*. Any member of either House — not just ministers — can introduce a bill if he or she so wishes. Bills issuing from non-ministerial MPs or peers are known as *private members' bills*. The various types of PMB will be considered later in the chapter, but it must at once be emphasised that *private members'* bills have no connection whatever with the *private bills* described above. On the contrary, PMBs are a type of *public* bill, and when introduced are subject to the same public bill procedure as government bills.

The legislative procedure for public bills

A bill may be introduced first into either the Commons or Lords. But in practice most government bills — and all those with major financial implications — start in the Commons, and the procedure set out below is for bills which start there. It is shown diagrammatically in Figure 5.1.

Drafting

All bills are presented to Parliament in the form of a complete draft statute. Except in 'emergency' cases, or in the first session after a government has taken office, the drafting of government bills begins long before they are laid before one of the Houses. The future legislation committee of the Cabinet decides which measures will make up the government's legislative programme for each session some months before it begins. In so doing it has to weigh the respective — and competing — claims of the party's election manifesto, departmental requirements and proposals for legislation carried in the reports of official committees and the like. Sometimes — particularly if their intentions are uncertain, or if they wish to gather informed opinion or 'test the water' — ministers issue a consultative paper (known as a *Green Paper*) before deciding on specific legislation; in addition, or instead, they may publish a statement of legislative intent (a *White Paper*). But it takes upwards of eighteen months to go through the entire Green Paper/White Paper/ drafting/bill process, and it is usually done only when the government is determined to act cautiously, which is usually when it fears it will meet resistance from important interested parties — as, for example, with the government's 1989 plans for radical reform of the NHS and the legal profession.

Once the session's legislative programme has been agreed, the relevant departments set about drawing up the bills, occasionally — with highly controversial bills — in conjunction with a Cabinet

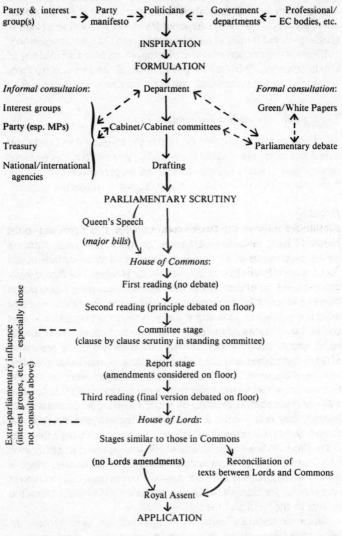

Figure 5.1 Principal stages in the legislative process for government bills

Source: Adapted from Table 7.1 of Gavin Drewry's 'Legislation' (in M. Ryle & P. G. Richards, *The Commons Under Scrutiny* (Routledge, 1988), pp. 124–5).

committee, and exceptionally (as with the 1987 poll tax proposals) with disputed points going to the full Cabinet. The formal drafting is the work of government legal officials called *Parliamentary Draftsmen* (or *Parliamentary Counsel*), who wield more influence over the shape of legislation than their title might suggest.

First reading

A major government bill will very likely be announced in the Queen's Speech. Whether it is or not, it will be introduced into the Commons soon after the opening of the session, whereupon it will be given a *first reading*. (The term 'reading' dates from the days before printing when bills were indeed 'read' to the House by a Clerk; now it refers simply to a stage through which a bill must pass.) The first reading is purely formal, with no debate. After it the bill is printed.

Second reading

About two weeks after a bill has been printed it goes through its first substantive stage – the *second reading*, when it is explained to the House and a debate takes place on its general principles. If these are contested there may be a vote at the end of the debate; and if the motion for the second reading is defeated, the bill proceeds no further. Private members' bills are often defeated at second reading, but government bills almost never fall at this stage since they are invariably subject to a three-line whip – and, anyway, opposition within the governing party's ranks is rarely to the principle, as opposed to the details, of a bill. The only government bill defeated on second reading in recent years was the 1986 Shops Bill. The bill, which sought to liberalise the Sunday trading laws, fell after sixty-eight Tory MPs joined the Opposition in voting against, with a further twenty abstaining. But it was a peculiar case of a second-tier issue which blew up unexpectedly when the church-led 'Keep Sunday Special' campaign agitated against the measure. Conservative MPs grew alarmed – not least since the party had given no previous manifesto commitment to legislate on Sunday trading – and the government half-acquiesced in the bill's demise. All in all, it was a highly exceptional affair.

Major bills are normally debated for one day on second reading but occasionally – as with the Water Bill, whose passage through Parliament is detailed below – the debate extends to two or more days. Immediately after the second reading is agreed, the Commons approves (usually without a vote) a financial resolution authorising the expenditure of any money 'for the purpose of any Act resulting from the ... Bill'.

Committee stage

At the committee stage a bill is examined in detail, clause by clause, by a *standing committee** of some twenty MPs. Members are chosen in proportion to the party balance in the House itself, with ministers from the promoting department and their Opposition 'shadows' always included. Depending on the type of bill, a standing committee can take anything from a few minutes to three months to consider a bill, with most major government bills requiring upwards of a dozen committee sittings of about three hours each spread over six weeks or more. From time to time – notably with the annual Finance Bill ('the Budget') and with bills involving major constitutional changes – all or part of a bill's committee stage is taken on the floor of the Commons where any MP can participate.

The effectiveness of standing committees will be considered in Chapter 7. Suffice it to note here that though committees can amend bills as they see fit, it is, in practice, exceptional for a committee to make major changes to a government bill against the wishes of the minister in charge. Committee stages of major bills are massively exhausting for all concerned; but for the most part their only concrete impact is a few weighty volumes of *Hansard* reports.

Report Stage

When a standing committee has completed its task, it 'reports' its bill to the House (usually, with major bills, sometime around Easter). This gives rise to the *report stage*, when further amendments can be proposed on the floor of the House – though with major bills only a few of the amendments tabled, selected by the Speaker, can be debated in the time available. A bill considered in a committee of the whole house and passed unamended goes straight to third reading, but that rarely happens. Depending on the bill in question, the report stage may take anything from a few minutes to several days.

Third Reading

The last hurdle a bill has to pass in the Commons is the *third reading*, when the text is debated in its final form. A vote may take place, but

* The Commons committee system is explained in Chapter 7.

it highly unusual for any kind of bill to be rejected at this late stage. Indeed, for all but controversial bills the third reading is a formality.

The government can restrict the time allowed for stages from committee onwards by using its majority to pass a *guillotine motion*, as explained on page 70.

House of Lords

Once a bill has passed the Commons it automatically proceeds to the Lords, where it goes through a broadly similar procedure. There are, however, three notable differences (elaborated in Chapter 10):

* The committee stage of public bills is normally taken on the floor of the Lords, not in a standing or select committee.

* There is no provision for curbing debate in the Lords.

* The Lords almost never votes on any of the readings of a government bill.

Once a bill has passed the Lords, any amendments made there go back to the Commons for consideration (if there are none, it is immediately submitted for the *Royal Assent*). The Commons can do one of three things with each Lords amendment: it may agree to it; it may substitute an amendment of its own; or it may disagree outright. If it opts for either of the last two courses with any amendments, the bill is returned to the Lords with 'reasons' for the Commons' actions. The Lords, in turn, may (and usually does) either accept the new Commons amendment(s) or agree not to insist on its amendment(s) rejected by the Commons. But if the peers decide to insist on any of their amendments, or suggest yet another version, more toing-and-froing goes on between the Houses in an attempt to reach agreement. Very exceptionally – and this has only happened on a handful of occasions since 1945, always with Labour governments – the two Houses cannot agree on a final text, and the bill therefore lapses. If that happens, the bill can be revived by the Commons in the following session and passed without the Lords' consent under the provisions of the 1911 and 1949 Parliament Acts.

Royal Assent

The Queen, as one of the branches of Parliament, must assent to all bills passed by the two Houses – or under the provisions of the Parliament Acts – before they can become law. The Royal Assent is now always a formality. Once it has been signified, the bill in question becomes an act, and is printed by HMSO both individually and in the annual series of Public and General Acts.

Application

Some bills come into force immediately after the Royal Assent; others on a date specified in the Act (there may be different dates for different parts); and others only after a *Commencement Order* has been issued by a minister (which may or may not be subject to parliamentary approval). An act may also give a minister – or other nominated persons or bodies – the power to make subsidiary rules or regulations which will have legal force; law so made is called *subordinate legislation*, and is explained later in the chapter.

Guillotine Motions

A *guillotine* – formally an 'allocation of time motion' – is a Commons motion regulating the time the House is prepared to allow itself or its committees to consider a particular bill. Guillotines are invariably moved by ministers dissatisfied with the progress one of their bills is making in standing committee, usually after it has proved impossible to reach a satisfactory agreement on future progress 'through the usual channels'. A guillotine rigidly allocates the time available for the outstanding stages of a bill; it has itself to be debated and voted upon by the full House, but only once since 1945 has a guillotine been defeated (over the 1976 Devolution Bill).

Guillotine motions date back to 1881, but they have been used with increasing frequency in recent years. In the 1987/8 session six bills were guillotined, the largest number ever in a single session. The Opposition always feels – or makes a show of feeling – aggrieved by their use. 'It cannot be denied', as Erskine May puts it, 'that they are capable of being used in such a way as to upset the balance, generally so carefully preserved, between the claims of business, and the rights of debate.' But for the most part guillotines have a negligible effect on the quality of Commons legislative scrutiny. Indeed, part of the reason for their increased use is a recent recommendation of the Procedure Committee to the effect that where progress on a measure was causing concern, some form of timetabling should be resorted to as early as possible to ensure adequate debate of all parts of a bill.

Timetable

How long does it take for a bill to become law?

In extremis both Houses can suspend Standing Orders and pass even the most important bill in a matter of hours if need be. The bill restoring direct rule to Northern Ireland, for example, was enacted in less than three days in 1972. Following normal procedures, however, even comparatively minor bills usually take several months to pass, extending to six months or more for controversial government bills (quite apart from the time previously required for drafting). There is, though, one clear limitation. No public bill can be carried over from one session to another, which imposes an upper limit of about eleven months.

Consider, for example, the privatisation and restructuring of the water industry in England and Wales, one of the government's major legislative projects of the 1988/9 session. Here is the chronology of the whole legislative process involved:

1987

May: Conservative election manifesto commits the party to 'return to the public the Water Authorities, leaving certain functions to a new National Rivers Authority' if it wins the election

June: Conservatives win the general election with overall majority of 102 in the House of Commons

[June 1987 to November 1988: first session of new Parliament; plans to privatise the water industry prepared by the Department of the Environment]

1988

22 November: Queen's Speech opening 1988/9 session announces: 'A Bill will be introduced for England and Wales to establish a National Rivers Authority and to provide for the sale of the utility functions of the water authorities'

23 November: Water Bill First Reading (no debate); bill printed

7 & 8 December: Second Reading carried (301 votes to 241) and financial resolution agreed after 11½-hour debate

1989

20 December 1988 to 7 March 1989: Bill considered by Standing Committee D (38 members plus chairman) for *c.* 140 hours over 35 sittings

6 February: Guillotine motion to timetable further Commons discussion carried (272 votes to 199)

21 March to 4 April: Report Stage: 17 hours over 4 sittings

4 April: Third Reading carried after 4-hour debate (319 votes to 227); bill sent to House of Lords

5 April: First Reading in Lords (no debate)

17 April: Second Reading agreed after 8-hour debate (no vote)

2 May to 23 May: Committee Stage — 62 hours over 8 sittings in a Committee of the Whole House

6 June to 13 June: Report Stage — 29 hours over 4 sittings

27 June: Third Reading and Motion to Pass agreed after 8-hour debate (no vote)

3 & 4 July: Commons consideration of Lords amendments (8 half-hours)

6 July: Lords agrees not to insist on its outstanding amendments with which the Commons has disagreed; Royal Assent signified

September: Establishment of the National Rivers Authority

November: Flotation of the ten new water companies

What difference does Parliament make?

The passage of the Water Bill took up almost 300 hours of parliamentary time spread over more than seven months. Yet for all that, *not one* amendment of any substance was made by either House. The sole change of any consequence — a Lords amendment which would have obliged the privatised water companies to achieve levels of drinking water quality specified by the European Community by 1993 — was reversed by the government's majority in the Commons and not insisted upon by the peers. It is fair to ask, therefore: is parliamentary scrutiny of government legislation anything more than 'sound and fury signifying nothing'?

It should first be remarked that there is nothing new in scepticism as to the value of parliamentary legislative scrutiny. And in so far as the scepticism is justified, it does not therefore follow that the system is a sham. The subordination of Parliament to the government of the day is a cornerstone of the British governmental system and ministers would not be in office at all if they did not command a majority of the Commons, usually from one party alone, prepared to support their legislative programme. More than twenty years ago S. A. Walkland wrote:

In so far as there is a 'deliberative' stage in the legislative process, this is now found much earlier than the Parliamentary stages, in the interplay between political parties, pressure groups, Departments and the Cabinet, which together form a complex decision making structure, involving a variety of social and political forces.

Legislation, it is thus argued, is the result of pressure from and bargaining between these groups. Parliament's role is one of *registration* and *legitimation*: it cloaks legislation agreed elsewhere with the form and force of law. Only in the rare cases (one since 1945) of minority administrations does Parliament play anything more than an incidental role in the deliberative process itself.

However, such a view underestimates Parliament's role. In particular, it fails to take account of the extent to which MPs are themselves one of the groups contending within the 'complex decision-making structure'. For MPs and peers — particularly the former — exert their own forms of pre-legislative pressure on governments, in four ways:

1. *Time*. One of the greatest constraints on a government's legislative ambitions is the amount of parliamentary time available to fulfil them. As it is, Parliament sits for about two-thirds of the year and ministers monopolise the time of the Commons — and, less formally, of the Lords as well. Yet the time required to enact a major measure — like the Water Bill above — is so great that no more than three or four such bills can be put forward each session. Ministers have no power comparable to that of the French government, which can enact a controversial bill in a matter of days, with the barest of parliamentary majorities, simply by invoking article 49 of the French constitution on its behalf, whereupon it is deemed to be passed unless an absolute majority of members of the National Assembly carry a motion of censure.

Governments could try to overcome the time constraint by introducing a version of the French article 49, or at least by further extending use of the guillotine. But neither option is politically feasible, and even if it were, there would still be the problem of the House of Lords. In recent decades the Lords has come to take its legislative duties seriously and it devotes a majority of its time to considering government bills; yet, as we shall see (Chapter 10) its procedures impose distinct limitations on the volume of legislation the peers can consider, and no government could easily induce the Lords to forego their rights of scrutiny.

2. *Size of government majority*. The size of a government's majority conditions both the measures it can put forward and the degree to which it will have to respond to criticism from its own backbenchers. With a small majority, ministers cannot afford even minimal dissent from

their own side; even without such dissent, the strain involved in ensuring that no mishaps during the multifarious stages through which a bill must pass itself acts as an inducement to caution. Again, the contrast with France is stark: French ministers can (by art. 44 of the constitution) insist on a single package vote on their own text of a bill with such amendments as they has proposed or accepted (*vote bloqué*) – a power which practically obviates the need for effective parliamentary management, however small the ministerial majority.

It is important to stress that though Mrs Thatcher's government has been freer than most from the constraints of time and majority, it has been exceptional in so being. The government has now (1990) had eleven sessions at its disposal, and for the past six has enjoyed three figure Commons majorities. But such a combination of longevity and massive majorities is unmatched by *any* other post-war government. In fact, even the Thatcher government has had occasionally to yield to backbench disaffection, though not on any issue of great consequence.

3. *'Feedback'*. Before a government introduces legislation, it is careful to gauge backbench sentiment. Commons debates, informal soundings by ministers and whips, reactions to Green and White Papers, reports of select and backbench committees – all alert the government to party feeling and likely difficulties. The impact of such 'feedback' cannot be quantified and is in any case variable: but – except perhaps immediately after an election, when legislative priorities have already been determined – it may be far from negligible. Of course, it is likely to be more significant the smaller the government's majority; but MPs increasingly see themselves as partners, not simply spectators, in the business of government, and expect to have a direct input when their party is in office.

4. *Criticism*. However pliant a government's majority, Parliament gives ministers nothing approaching the power to legislate by decree. The procedure for passing bills is not only lengthy; it obliges ministers to explain, defend and justify their measures against destructive and constructive criticism – for months on end, if they are controversial. 'What we do not know', as Gavin Drewry has put it, 'is how often an idea fails ... simply because a minister shrinks from having to justify an unpopular policy in public. Herein lies much of Parliament's real influence, though because of its invisibility we can never measure its magnitude.'

Private members' bills (PMBs)

Whatever the theory, in practice, non-ministerial MPs — called 'private members' in parliamentary jargon — have only limited opportunities for introducing legislation. There are, in fact, four means by which they can do so.

Ballot bills

At the start of each session the names of twenty MPs are drawn in a ballot for the right to introduce a private member's bill on one of the twelve Friday sittings set aside for that purpose. In fact, only the first six of these sittings are reserved for second readings, the remaining days being largely devoted to the later stages of bills which have been through committee. Only the first six or so MPs are thus assured even of an opportunity for a debate on their bills — and without time for debate, the chances of a bill making any headway are negligible.

Not all private members' bills are serious attempts to change the law; many are simply propaganda exercises. Ballot bills — or at least those introduced by MPs high in the ballot — are usually serious in intent, but even so they invariably need at least tacit government support to be successful. Without it they may well fall at second reading, and if not at that stage, then through obstruction or defeat later. In their detailed study of PMBs, Marsh and Read emphasise the fact that not since 1959 has a PMB subject to a vote on the floor of the Commons passed without government time, and conclude that 'most [are] Government bills in all but name'. Ministers, for their part, treat PMBs as useful devices for legislating on matters — particularly social issues with strong 'moral' overtones — which they are reluctant to tackle with official policy and the rigours of the whipping system. PMBs may thus embrace controversial issues: the so-called 'permissive society' legislation of the 1960s — the abolition of the death penalty, the legalisation of homosexuality and the permitting and regulating of abortion — was largely enacted by means of PMBs; and more recently legislation on issues such as female circumcision and child abuse has been enacted by PMBs. A fair proportion of PMBs are, therefore, as much the handiwork of the government as of the MPs initiating them.

Ten-minute rule bills

With appropriate notice any MP can introduce a bill in a specially reserved twenty-minute slot after Question Time on each Tuesday and

Wednesday after the sixth week of the session. The sponsor is permitted a ten-minute speech of introduction, to which a ten-minute speech of opposition can be made by an MP who 'catches the Speaker's eye'. There may then be a division on the bill.

'Ten-minute' bills have one advantage over ballot bills: they are introduced in prime media time. Competition to introduce them is thus intense, and the slots are allocated on a 'first-come-first-served' basis about three weeks in advance. For the most part ten-minute bills are little more than publicity gimmicks: even if they pass the initial hurdle, they join the ballot bill queue for a second reading and rarely see the light of day again (fewer than twenty-five have become law since 1945). To take a month at random, the ten-minute bills introduced in February 1989 included a Labour proposal to amend the 'poll tax', and Tory proposals to abolish age discrimination in employment, to increase competition in the sale of books and to remove the Post Office's monopoly on letter delivery (the latter opposed and voted down by 174 to 100).

Standing Order 58 bills

Standing Order 58 procedure is similar to that for 'ten-minute' bills, with two additional drawbacks: bills introduced under SO58 are not debated at all at their introduction, and thus attract virtually no publicity. Perhaps because of this, the success rate for SO 58 bills is marginally higher than for 'ten-minute' bills (one such bill exceptionally passed through all its stages in the Commons in 67 seconds in July 1976). But this simply reflects the fact that MPs have nothing to gain from introducing any but the most anodyne of measures under the procedure.

Private peers' bills

Backbench members of the House of Lords can introduce bills with greater freedom than MPs; but even if their bills pass the Lords, they stand little chance of being considered by the Commons unless entirely uncontroversial. Of the twenty-five private peers' bills passed by the Lords between 1983 and 1986, for example, only ten reached the statute book. A number were designed to gain publicity rather than to result in legislation. The sponsor of one such bill in 1989, which sought to restrict the hours of junior hospital doctors to seventy-two a week, openly acknowledged that it stood no chance of passing, but had nonetheless served 'a useful purpose in raising public awareness of the current situation'.

Assessment

Some fifteen private members' or private peers' bills reach the statute book each session (see Table 5.1). Perhaps they serve to keep alive the idea that legislation emanates from Parliament as a whole, not just from the government of the day. If so, it is a misleading impression, for in practice they simply underline the fact that no bill has any serious chance of becoming law without at least tacit government support. PMBs are, however, more than simply an addition to the government's legislative armoury. They provide an important mechanism enabling the major parties, between them, to agree on legislation affecting delicate social and moral issues while respecting the consciences of backbenchers and keeping their leaders free of binding commitments. Considering the difficulties experienced by other democracies in handling such matters, their utility should not be underestimated.

Table 5.1   Private members' bills, 1983–87 Parliament

	Ballot	10-min. rule	SO58	Private peers	Total
Total introduced	79	195	107	60	441
Not printed	3	78	11	0	92
One reading	13	111	77	9	210
2nd rdg lost/adjourned	18	3	4	8	33
Royal Assent	39	2	13	14	68
% success rate	49	1	12	23	15

Private legislation

Erskine May defines private legislation as 'legislation of a special kind for conferring particular powers or benefits on any person or body of persons ... in excess of or in conflict with the general law'. In practice, most private bills are promoted by corporate bodies like local authorities or companies for the purpose of acquiring specific legal powers.

Until the early nineteenth century, private and public legislation were of at least equal importance. The large-scale enclosure of farming land and the building of canals and railways — all three heralding dramatic social and economic changes – were accomplished by means of thousands of separate private acts. But as central government came increasingly to plan and provide for such matters on a national scale, the role of private legislation rapidly diminished. Nowadays a few dozen private bills at most are enacted each session, and consideration of them occupies barely 3% of parliamentary time. Nonetheless, their importance has revived in recent years as developers have increasingly come to use them as an alternative to the planning process for securing consents for large-scale developments. In the past decade a number of major container terminals, private docks, marinas and the like have been built under powers acquired by private acts.

Private bills are subject to a very different procedure from public bills. In the first place, they are presented not by an MP or a peer but by a 'promoter' (the individual or body requesting the legislation) who is represented by lawyers known as parliamentary agents. After their second reading in each House, private bills go to a select committee which sits like a court and decides – with legal assistance – whether the powers sought are in order and conform with precedent. Any individual directly affected by a proposed development may petition against it; and if a bill is thus opposed, the committee hears evidence and statements (usually put forward by barristers) from promoters and objectors before deciding whether to refuse, amend or agree the bill in question.

A small number of bills are classed as both 'public' and 'private' because of their provisions, a notable recent example being the 1987 Channel Tunnel Bill. Such bills are termed *hybrid* and treated as if public bills, except that, in addition to their usual committee stage, they are referred to a private bill committee in each House for consideration of 'private' objections (over 1,000 petitions were lodged against the Channel Tunnel Bill). The government does not normally take a stand on private bills and most go unopposed on the floors of the two Houses. But if a single MP or peer objects, a private bill must be debated – which can result in it being lost due to pressure of time, although private (unlike public) bills can be carried forward from one session to the next.

The private bill system has been the subject of considerable recent criticism. It is argued that the procedure is outdated, that it allows wealthy individuals or corporations to subvert the established planning process, and that it is too secretive and unduly restrictive in its interpretation of the rights of objectors to developments. From

Parliament's point of view it is also expensive: each bill costs about £10,000 to consider, only a small fraction of which is recovered in fees charged to developers. Concern grew to such a level in the mid-1980s that in 1987 a joint select committee of MPs and peers was established to investigate the whole private bill system. It reported in favour of:

* reducing the scope of private legislation by restricting it to matters which cannot be handled in any other way;

* providing for public − as well as parliamentary − enquiries into bills with substantial planning implications; and

* granting wider powers to ministers − subject to established constraints − in public legislation to reduce the need for private bills.

But the government's response to the report was lukewarm and no changes to the private bill system are in prospect.

Delegated legislation

Delegated legislation − also known as secondary or subordinate legislation − is legislation issued under authority conferred (or 'delegated') for the purpose by statute. To take a simple example, the 1968 Gaming Act stipulates the maximum winnings allowed at bingo and gives the Home Secretary power to raise the figure by delegated legislation; the Highway Code and the Immigration Rules have force by the same means. Power to make delegated legislation is usually given to ministers, but it is sometimes granted to bodies such as local authorities or nationalised industries. Generally speaking, it is used for specialised and detailed matters, typically to provide for regulations implementing specific provisions (like the poll tax and state benefits), particularly those liable to change over time. Delegated legislation thus confers extensive powers on ministers and other public officials, and forms a significant component of the law of the land.

Delegated legislation takes a variety of forms. The most important is the *Statutory Instrument (SI)*. Some 2,000 SIs are issued each year. About half are of purely local application and subject to no parliamentary oversight; the rest fall into three categories:

* *General instruments*. These are in the main uncontentious, and are laid before Parliament merely for information. Some seventy general instruments are issued each year.

* *Affirmative instruments*. Some acts stipulate that particular SIs made under them must receive affirmative approval by Parliament within a specified period, usually twenty-eight or forty days. In

exceptional circumstances, an 'affirmative' SI might come into force as soon as issued, ceasing to have effect if not approved within the required time. About 170 affirmative instruments are laid before Parliament each year; most require the approval of both Houses, but those relating solely to financial matters are the concern of the Commons alone.

* *Negative instruments*. About 900 'negative instruments' are laid before Parliament each year; for the most part they take effect automatically after forty days unless either House passes a motion, called a 'prayer', to annul them.

SIs requiring parliamentary approval are examined by two committees: most of them go to the *Joint Committee on Statutory Instruments*, but those needing to be laid before the Commons alone go to the *Commons Select Committee on Statutory Instruments* (which is simply the Commons members of the joint committee). The function of the committees is purely technical: to determine whether each SI conforms to its 'parent' act.

There can be no question as to the necessity for delegated legislation. Erskine May talks of its 'speed, flexibility and adaptability', particularly valuable in spheres where ministers or public bodies have continually to adapt the operation of statutes to changing conditions. But the shortcomings in parliamentary oversight of Statutory Instruments are flagrant:

1. *The SI committee*. If the SI committee is concerned that an Order may not conform to the letter or intent of its 'parent' act, or if it wishes to have further elucidation, then it can report the offending Order to the House. But the committee is not itself permitted to consider the merits of SIs; and even where it reports that an Order goes beyond the terms of its parent act, the House is not obliged to act on the report, nor is the government required to give reasons for repudiating it.

2. *Lack of Commons debates*. Hardly any time is made available to debate SIs on the floor of the Commons, and if they are debated at all it is usually late at night or in the early hours of the morning and for a strictly limited time. The exception is subordinate legislation affecting Northern Ireland, much of it enacted by *Orders in Council*, a form of SI, which are rather better debated.

3. *Inability to amend SIs*. An SI cannot be amended on the floor of either Commons or Lords, or in a committee. It must either be rejected or accepted as a whole, unless the threat of rejection wrings amendments from the government (which, being a hollow threat, it virtually never does).

4. *Scope of SIs*. SIs have come increasingly to be used by ministers to make new policy and not simply to enact detailed rules within an existing policy, a trend which neither House has seriously attempted to thwart. The judiciary is so concerned at this trend that, in a remarkable development in judicial review, the Court of Appeal in 1989 overrode a Statutory Instrument which in its view failed to fulfil the provisions of its parent act.* 'The implied invitation thus to challenge such delegated legislation in the court', wrote a leading commentator, 'should serve notice on politicians that more careful scrutiny is needed at Westminster.'

Parliament and lobbyists

Lobbyists have always been an integral part of parliamentary life. For as long as businesses, interests and individuals have been concerned – directly, vicariously or altruistically – with the law, they have sought to influence its form and operation. The diversity of interest groups in contemporary Britain, everything from Friends of the Earth and the Stock Exchange through to Upper Marshland Parish Council, is matched only by the diversity of their lobbying techniques. 'Keep Sunday Special' campaigned against the 1986 Shops Bill by inviting MPs to special church meetings up and down the land; the National Union of Students periodically organises mass Westminster lobbies of thousands of students to oppose whatever is the higher education policy of the day; companies operate more subtly through professional consultants, or have their own contacts with individual MPs; while

---

* *McKiernon* v. *Secretary of State for Social Security*. It concerned a section of the Social Securities Act 1975 which declares that regulations may modify entitlement to disablement benefit, and another providing that regulations should allow for an extension in the claim period if good reason for delay can be shown by the claimant. The SI contested by McKiernon laid down a time limit for claims, but made no provision for 'good cause' extensions. The Court ruled that this constituted a modification of the original act, which was not expressly stated as such in the SI; it therefore referred the case back to the DSS. However, it avoided ruling on the principle of modifications to acts made by SIs.

aggrieved residents of Upper Marshland might turn up in Central Lobby and send in a 'green card' asking to speak to their MP. All alike are lobbying Parliament; and all alike intend their action to procure some benefit or change in a law or administrative decision.

Not that by any means all political lobbying is directed at Parliament. Many interest groups focus their activities on Whitehall, local government or the political parties directly. Conversely, many interest groups are themselves consulted by officials, ministers and politicians, and may have a direct input into legislation long before it comes to the notice of Commons or Lords. The 1980s have, nonetheless, seen a marked increase in the volume and sophistication of parliamentary lobbying, which can be assessed under five headings:

1. *Direct lobbying*. Interest groups are increasingly keen to establish a 'presence' at Westminster, often through a lobbyist with direct access to, and contacts with, MPs. In 1988 it was estimated that some fifty individuals, nominally on the staff of MPs, had Commons entry passes indicating a connection with a parliamentary consultancy or public relations firm, with another fifty employed by charities, professional bodies or other non-profit-making organisations. The House of Commons Service Committee recently reported (2nd report, 1987/8) that it had received 'disturbing evidence' of direct approaches from lobbying organisation to MPs 'in some cases blatantly seeking the issue of a House of Commons photo-identity pass as a cover for commercial lobbying activities in return for 'services' to the member concerned'. One MP forwarded a letter from a public affairs consultancy requesting a pass in these terms: 'With the position of lobbyists being a rather grey area, I would suggest that a pass be issued under the guise of a research appointment. In order to make this above-board, but also to give you something in return for sponsoring a Pass, I am prepared to undertake any work for you.' The committee believed such evidence to be 'the tip of a large iceberg, and one whose progress should be halted'.

2. *Support for MPs*. It would be wrong to see MPs as invariably the unwilling victims of interest-group pressure. On the contrary, in much of their parliamentary work interest groups are in fact *assisting* MPs sympathetic to their cause in the first place – particularly Opposition spokesmen having to confront the might of Whitehall with only a few researchers and a secretary apiece and ever in search of new sticks with

which to beat the government. More generally, MPs support the activities of constituency and other interest groups, from organised and well-financed affairs (like the Kent group which successfully fought British Rail's planned route for the new Channel Tunnel rail link in 1989) to the more humdrum efforts of parish councils or residents' associations. Furthermore, MPs promoting private members' bills are often heavily reliant on interest groups, if not for the idea of the bill in the first place then for help in its preparation. In the 1989 *Register of Members' Interests*, for example, David Alton listed 'research assistance and secretarial help' for his Abortion Bill from three groups: CARE (Christian, Action, Research and Education), SPUC (Society for the Protection of the Unborn Child) and LIFE.

3. *Commercial lobbyists*. Specialist commercial lobbying of MPs and peers has expanded markedly in recent years. There are now more than forty firms, many of them engaging the services of MPs and peers themselves (see below), which specialise in providing governmental and parliamentary PR services. Most of their clients are businesses: a 1985 survey of 180 large British companies found that 41% employed government affairs consultants and 28% employed PR companies for work involving government.

4. *MPs as lobbyists*. The number of MPs who are themselves consultants or lobbyists, often for substantial financial rewards, has escalated in the 1980s. In the 1989 *Register of Members' Interests*, one in three of all non-ministerial MPs (191 in total) is listed as an 'adviser', 'consultant' or director of a public relations firm, with many listing more than one such post. The range of organisations served by MPs is considerable, from companies, trade and professional associations and PR consultancy firms through to the National Bedding Federation (Elizabeth Peacock), the National Hairdressers' Federation (John Hunt), the British Fur Trade Association (Gwyneth Dunwoody) and the National Tyre Distributors' Association (Iain Mills). It is unclear precisely what 'services' are provided by MPs, but it is notable that the 'consultants' and 'advisers' are predominantly Tories* (though

---

* According to Jordan and Richardson, 'One of the powers of the Whip over potential rebels in the party is a threat to try to keep them off Select Committees and out of other activities which would be important for their consultancy work.' This clearly applies more to Tory than to Labour MPs.

almost half of all Labour MPs are sponsored by trade unions and expected to maintain at least a 'watching brief' on matters affecting their interests). Former MPs are also more than ready to make their knowledge and contacts available – usually for a fee. One casualty of the 1987 election (Alf Dubs) has even published a book entitled *Lobbying: An Insider's Guide to the Parliamentary Process*.

5. *The House of Lords.* The 1980s have also seen an extension of lobbying activity to the Lords. As the peers have come to play an active role in the legislative process, even occasionally (and more frequently than MPs) upsetting ministerial proposals, lobbyists have learnt to take them seriously for the first time. Single-issue groups are particularly active in briefing peers, with 'social' groups like Shelter and Help the Aged eager to help Opposition spokesmen in the Lords – obliged to be even more self-reliant than their Commons counterparts – with research and drafting assistance. There appears also to be a growing tendency for peers themselves to act as lobbyists, either for payment or from direct interest. This came publicly to the fore in 1986, when the Labour peer Lord Northfield introduced a Patents (Amendment) Bill. Northfield's position as a pharmaceuticals consultant compromised his attempt to tighten up the laws relating to patents on new drugs – not least when, after the debate, it transpired that almost all of those taking part had at some stage worked in the pharmaceuticals industry or as a patent lawyer. This and other similar incidents caused such concern that the issue was investigated by a Lords committee in 1987, which recommended that 'the rules about the declaration of Peers' interests should be stricter and clearer ... A Lord should not advocate or oppose legislation if he has received a pecuniary reward in relation to it.' Noble sentiments, but as yet no action has been taken.

Does lobbying make a difference?

Parliamentary lobbying is often considered to be a waste of time, since all important administrative and legislative decisions are taken in Whitehall. On this reading, parliamentary lobbyists are either ignorant, foolhardy, or, if neither, *obliged* to lobby MPs and peers because they lack 'access' to the formative stages of the decision-making process (see Figure 5.1). There is some truth in all three explanations, perhaps particularly the third. But it would be a mistake to dismiss parliamentary lobbying out of hand. First, it often serves as an indirect – or complementary – means of lobbying Whitehall itself. The 1985 survey mentioned in 3 above supports this: 69% of the 180 large firms surveyed saw a need for monitoring Whitehall, compared with 61% for monitoring Parliament; but whereas only 8% of those employing consultants saw them as useful for gaining access to Whitehall, 60% believed them to be satisfactory so far as MPs were concerned. Through MPs, interest groups hope to reach ministers and officials, and often do so.

Secondly, interest groups are by no means always concerned to influence *specific* proposals or decisions; they are often just as concerned to influence the climate of opinion. As Jordan and Richardson put it in their study of pressure groups and government in modern Britain:

Groups ... pay attention to Parliament − inspire questions, give evidence to Select Committees, brief MPs − because even when actual legislative change is not in sight the groups can hope to put matters on the political agenda, stimulate interest in their problems, and establish their reputation and credibility as expert sources of views in their field. Parliament can be helpful in 'climate setting', even where immediate and direct legislative benefit cannot be seen.

Which brings us full circle. The legislative process is complex and multi-faceted; concentration on the formal stages through which bills have to pass gives a distorted impression and ignores the dynamic role of Parliament in the process.

6

Questions and debates in the House of Commons

The making of legislation is only one role of the House of Commons. As the 'Grand Inquest of the Nation' its other major functions are to deliberate on matters of public interest and to keep a check on the activities of the executive. Beyond that, MPs have duties to those who elected them in the first place – to pursue constituents' interests and to take up their grievances. For these purposes the Commons spends a significant proportion of its time debating and questioning ministers; indeed (see Figure 6.1), the Commons spends longer on debates and questions than on any other activity. This chapter outlines the format of questions and debates and assesses their effectiveness for the purposes of scrutiny and deliberation. At the end it considers the likely impact of the televising of Commons proceedings on these and other aspects of its work.

Questions

According to Erskine May, parliamentary questions have two main objectives: 'to obtain information or to press for action'. Beyond that, they also serve as prominent weapons in the party political battle. Question Time is the best reported part of Commons business; front-benchers and backbenchers alike use it to score party points and to draw attention to themselves and their causes.

Questions have long been an integral part of Commons business. The first oral questions were asked in the mid-eighteenth century; by the early nineteenth century they had become an established device for eliciting information from ministers; and in 1869 the institution of Question Time was established in something like its modern form. The two most significant changes since then have been the introduction of

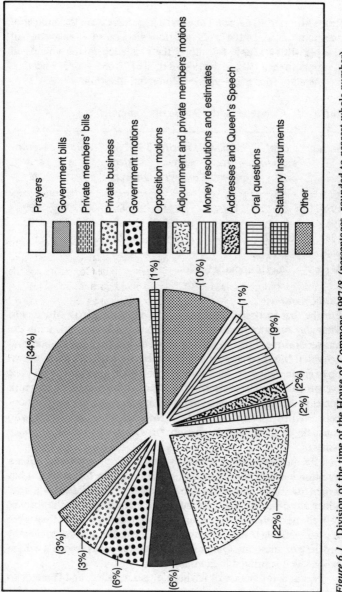

Figure 6.1 Division of the time of the House of Commons 1987/8 (percentages, rounded to nearest whole number)

Prayers
Government bills
Private members' bills
Private business
Government motions
Opposition motions
Adjournment and private members' motions
Money resolutions and estimates
Addresses and Queen's Speech
Oral questions
Statutory Instruments
Other

(1%)
(34%)
(3%)
(3%)
(6%)
(6%)
(22%)
(2%)
(2%)
(9%)
(1%)
(10%)

Prime Minister's Question Time and a huge increase in the number of questions tabled. In 1847, 129 questions were asked – an average of one per sitting; Table 6.1 shows the escalation in the volume of questions in the 1980s, to the 1987/8 total of 72,666 – or 333 per day.

There are four main types of Commons question.

Table 6.1   Questions in the House of Commons

Session	Oral answers	Ordinary written answers	Priority written answers	Total for written answers	Total	Average per sttg day
1980/1	8,175	11,634	11,054	22,688	30,863	189
1985/6	18,139	12,548	19,260	31,808	49,947	290
1987/8*	24,940	20,750	26,976	47,726	72,666	333

Note: * Long (16-month) session

Oral Questions

For the first forty to fifty minutes of every sitting from Monday to Thursday (usually from around 2.45 p.m. to 3.30 p.m.), ministers answer oral questions put to them about their departmental duties and activities. Ministers appear before the House on a rota basis, drawn up to ensure that each department is exposed to questions about once every three to four weeks during the session. When a department's turn comes up, all of its Commons ministers appear and divide the questions between them – with the minister at the head of the department (who is usually in the Cabinet) generally answering only on major policy issues.

MPs must give at least two days' notice of oral questions. After a question has been asked and the answer given, the MP putting it has a right to a further unscripted question (called a 'supplementary'), after which any other MP may continue the interrogation until the Speaker calls the next question. Since far more questions are tabled than there is time available to answer them, MPs enter a ballot to determine the ordering of questions. Questions not answered orally receive a written reply which is printed in *Hansard*.

To stand any chance of having a question called, an MP needs to table it at the maximum permissible notice of ten sitting days (i.e. two weeks, in effect) before the Question Time concerned. Partly because of that, and partly to broaden the scope for raising topical matters in supplementaries – the most lively aspect of Question Time – MPs are tending increasingly to table open-ended questions like: 'What representations has the Chancellor of the Exchequer received from political parties for increases in public expenditure?', and 'Has the Chancellor any estimate of the cost to the Exchequer of the present level of unemployment in Liverpool?'

However, far more is involved in Question Time than simply the seeking and giving of information. Ministerial reputations are won and lost by dexterity at the Despatch Box, and backbenchers and Opposition spokesmen keen to make their mark pay especial attention to their performance in the 'battle of the supplementaries'.

Prime Minister's questions

Questions to the Prime Minister formally enjoy the same status as any other oral or written questions, but in practice they are a class apart. Since 1961 the Prime Minister has answered questions for fifteen minutes at 3.15 p.m. each Tuesday and Thursday during the session. These two short periods are the high points of the parliamentary week, especially the exchanges between the Prime Minister and Leader of the Opposition. The Chamber is always packed to capacity and the half-hour usually attracts more public and media attention than all the rest of the week's parliamentary business put together.

Most questions to the Prime Minister take the form: 'To ask the Prime Minister if she will list her official engagements for [the day of the sitting]'. These open questions allow the questioner to ask a supplementary about almost anything topical, and require the Prime Minister to be briefed and able to reply. The Leader of the Opposition is – uniquely – allowed three questions, and the other party leaders often take part too. 'Who came out on top' is a talking point of MPs and journalists for much of the day after.

Prime Minister's Question Time is a peculiarly British institution. In no other major democracy except Canada does the Head of Government have to appear so regularly in Parliament to answer questions and reply to criticism, still less to do battle on equal terms with other party leaders. In the United States, for example, the President appears in Congress only once a year – to deliver his State of the Union address – and is never subjected to Congressional questioning. In Britain, by contrast, a commanding presence in the Commons has always been essential to a Prime Minister's standing in his or her party and – via the media – in the country at large, however large his or her ostensible majority. 'No Prime Minister looks forward to "PQs" with anything but apprehension', Lord Wilson (the former Labour Prime Minister) has written. Harold Macmillan, Conservative Prime Minister from 1957 to 1963, rated performance in the Commons above almost all the other challenges he faced; Horne records an interview with him in which he remarked: 'I didn't worry ... I didn't even mind losing a by-election or bother too much with the outside world, if you can once impress upon the House of Commons that the Government is strong and the Prime Minister is in control ... then gradually ... it begins to go out into the country ...'.

As an insight into the ways of the Commons, the debating skills required in a Prime Minister, and the contrast between formal and informal modes of behaviour in the House, nothing betters Macmillan's description of how he handled questions:

you have to know the man who is your questioner ... like a prep school, there are boys who are popular, whom you must never slap down, even if they are asking a silly question ... then there are the unpopular, the tiresome, and the House rather enjoys their being slapped down ... You must remember that, like a school, on the whole it dislikes the front bench (the masters) ... often you can turn an enemy into a friend, by some slight recognition.

Always keep your temper ... and always have a good control of questions and supplementaries ... in many ways this is the most anxious work; I would never have lunched out on question day.

Prime Minister's Question Time thus occupies a central place in Commons business. Gerald Kaufman's advice on *How to be a Minister* included the tip: 'instruct your Diary Secretary to put the Prime Minister's Question Time as a permanent engagement in your diary. You should also do your best to attend all the major debates in which the Prime Minister speaks.'

Questions for written answer

The vast majority of parliamentary questions are tabled for written answer. Replies to them are printed, together with the questions, in *Hansard*. This normally takes about a week, but MPs requiring answers on a specific day can designate their question(s) for 'priority written answer' and (see Table 6.1) this has become more popular than the non-priority question. MPs are limited to eight oral questions each per fortnight; but they can ask an unlimited number of questions for written answer.

Private Notice Questions

It is possible, with the consent of the Speaker, to raise matters of urgency at the end of Question Time by means of a Private Notice Question. Some four or five PNQs are asked each month in the session.

The Treasury estimates that it costs an average of £75 to answer an oral question and £45 a written question, and ministers often express concern at the total sums involved in the process (about £4 million in recent sessions). But this works out at about £28 per MP per sitting day — not, perhaps, an unjustifiably large price to pay for protecting the right of MPs to interrogate ministers. In any case, there is a ceiling of £250 on the cost of answering a question, and individual questions are sometimes met with the reply: 'The department does not have that information and it would be unjustifiably expensive to obtain.'

Table 6.2 Cost of question in the Commons

	Cost (£-1987 prices)	Cost per MP per sitting day (£)
1980/1	1,634,085	15
1985/6	2,791,785	25
1987/8	4,018,170	28

Numerous rules govern what may and may not be asked in questions. Ministers may not be questioned about matters beyond their direct responsibility, including the operational affairs of a nationalised industry. Issues which are the subject of judicial proceedings (*sub judice*) cannot be raised. Neither the Royal Family, the judiciary nor the Speaker can be criticised, except in a formal motion for the purpose. Finally, a minister is not obliged to answer any question, nor to give a reason for refusing to do so. Questions on some subjects — like the security services — are invariably met with silence; and even if a minister does answer, he cannot be prevented from being evasive — though he may have to defend himself against strong criticism if he is.

Impact of questions

1. *Obtaining information*. Of the three purposes listed at the outset
− obtaining information, pressing for action and waging the party
struggle − the first is now arguably the least important. It persists
to the extent that MPs may not find it possible to elicit certain
information in any other way. Beyond that, the attraction of PQs
lies in their official status, which most alternative published sources
lack. In addition, MPs often find it more convenient to use the
resources of government to do their research than to do it themselves.

2. *Pressing for action*. Questions are of greater value as a means
of drawing attention to a particular issue, and with the publicity
they attract they can be an effective means of provoking action.
At any rate, they enable Members to be *seen* to be pressing for
action by constituents and party colleagues. The most celebrated
use of questions for this purpose in recent years was the long-running
campaign waged by the Labour MP Tam Dalyell to uncover 'the
truth' about the sinking of the Argentinian battleship *General Belgrano*
during the 1982 Falklands War. Over the following three years
Dalyell tabled several hundred questions concerning the *Belgrano*'s
location and direction-of-sail prior to its destruction. Dalyell made
little headway, but in the process managed to provoke a *cause
célèbre* when, in July 1984, a senior Ministry of Defence official
− Clive Ponting − leaked him secret documents which appeared
to contradict earlier ministerial statements in the Commons. The
source of the leak was traced and Ponting prosecuted for a breach
of the Official Secrets Act; he was acquitted − but the precise
information requested by Dalyell has never been revealed.* Perhaps
such results account for MORI's finding that only 35% of Opposition
MPs regard questions as an 'effective' means of scrutiny, compared
to 59% of Conservatives.

---

* Dalyell has, however, been successful on other occasions. Denis Healey
  records that when he was Defence Secretary in the late 1960s the Defence
  Ministry planned to construct an Indian Ocean airbase on Aldabra (off
  Mozambique). 'Since it [Aldabra] was inhabited only by giant tortoises,
  frigate birds, and the great booby, we expected no political difficulties.
  We reckoned without the environmental lobby ... aided by a brilliant
  campaign of parliamentary questions from the assiduous Tam Dalyell.'

3. *Political battle.* The usefulness of questions as instruments in the party battle is disputed. Some argue that their value is limited given the length of time set aside for oral questions and MPs' inability to compel ministers to be more forthcoming than they wish to be. However, on a broader view of the party struggle, questions are invaluable. It has been said that a principal role of the House of Commons is to provide a battleground for the waging of an ongoing general election campaign. This role is of critical importance, serving as it does continually to bring home to the electorate the rights and wrongs of the political issues in dispute between the parties. Oral questions, particularly Prime Minister's Questions, are essential weapons in the battle, for government and Opposition alike.

Debates

More than a third of the time of the Commons is spent in debates. They take a number of forms:

1. *Debate on the Queen's Speech.* At the start of each new session of Parliament the first business of the House of Commons is a full-scale debate on the government's programme, as set out in the Queen's Speech. The debate is the longest of the session, spanning six or so sittings and ranging over the whole scope of government policy. It is also one of the few debates each session in which the Prime Minister participates. Indeed, about a quarter of the entire Commons, including a dozen or so ministers, customarily take part in the debate on the Queen's Speech.

At the end of the debate, votes take place on one or more Opposition amendment(s) to the ministerial programme. These votes are treated as motions of confidence: if the government fails to secure a majority in any of them, it is obliged either to resign immediately or to call an election. Only once this century has a government in fact been defeated on the Gracious Speech – in 1924, when Baldwin's Conservative government met Parliament as the largest party, but without a majority, and was defeated by Labour and Liberal MPs combined. Baldwin resigned and Ramsay MacDonald took office as the first Labour Prime Minister.

2. *Motions of no confidence.* From time to time the Opposition may table a motion of censure against the government, usually in the form:

'That this House has no confidence in Her Majesty's Government'. If carried, such a motion obliges the government either to resign or to call a general election. 'No confidence' motions are debated regularly when a government has only a small Commons majority, but otherwise they are relatively rare. Only one government this century has been defeated on a formal motion of no confidence, James Callaghan's in March 1979 (which lost the critical division by 311 votes to 310). The government was driven to an election at a time not of the Prime Minister's choice — and it lost.

3. *Government motions*. Some twenty days per session are devoted to debates on government motions, either annual debates on such subjects as the armed services and foreign affairs or on motions asking the Commons to 'note' new policy proposals.

4. *Opposition days*. Twenty days of each session are allocated to the Opposition. The Shadow Cabinet decides the topics to be debated on almost all of them (one or two are passed on to the smaller parties), and it often divides each of its days into two to maximise use of the available time. Opposition spokesmen open and close the debates; ministers from the relevant departments respond to the Opposition's case and generally move a government amendment supporting ministerial policy in the field in question, which is invariably carried at the end of the debate. To take a typical example, in February 1989 Neil Kinnock used an Opposition day to move a motion condemning the government's 'failure to fulfil its duty of care and safeguard the quality of food and water in Britain'. Kenneth Clarke, the Health Secretary, responded by moving an amendment deleting the substance of the motion and calling on the House instead to express its 'complete confidence' in government policy. After a six-hour debate, Mr Clarke's amendment was carried by 287 votes to 199.

5. *Adjournment debates and private members' motions*. At the end of each sitting the motion is moved: 'that the House do adjourn', whereupon a Member is free to make a speech on virtually any topic over which the government has responsibility. Only one such 'adjournment debate' takes place each sitting; it lasts for no more than half an hour, with a junior minister from the relevant department replying within that time. Competition for the thirty-minute slots is intense and a ballot is held every Thursday to allocate four for the following week

(the fifth is in the gift of the Speaker, who normally grants it to an MP consistently unsuccessful in the ballot). Subjects of adjournment debates vary greatly; but they are frequently used to air constituents' grievances of one kind or another. To give some idea of their range, here is the list of issues raised in the week beginning 17 July 1989. Notice, incidentally, the hours at which the House adjourns − a telling commentary on the absurd hours kept by MPs.

17 July	3.48 a.m.	Dave Nellist (Lab)	Homeless Young People (London)
18 July	10.12 p.m.	Harry Greenway (Con)	Airport Congestion
19 July	1.06 a.m.	Donald Anderson (Lab)	Swansea Submarine Base
20 July	11.25 p.m.	Teddy Taylor (Con)	Mr Jens Soering (Extradition)
21 July	2.09 p.m.	Ron Davies (Lab)	Nature Conservation and Wildlife

Apart from the adjournment, backbenchers have two other regular opportunities to initiate debates. Eleven days each session − mostly Fridays − are set aside for private members' motions, with the choice of subjects left to the MPs successful in a ballot. And the day and night before the House goes into recess are normally given over to backbenchers to initiate short debates, providing a further seven or so days for private members' motions.

6. *Emergency debates*. After Question Time each day a Member may make an oral request to the Speaker (lasting no more than three minutes) for time on the following day to initiate a debate on a matter which is 'specific and important and should have urgent consideration' (Standing Order No. 20). Rarely are more than one or two of the sixty-odd requests for emergency debates are allowed by the Speaker each session; but simply making an application ensures prime-time media attention − hence the popularity of the device, especially on the Opposition benches.

Conduct of Debate

Nothing better exemplifies the dominance of government and Opposition in the House of Commons than the conduct of debates. Almost all major debates are opened by a minister of a 'shadow' spokesman, who is invariably followed by a member of the opposite front bench; and debates similarly conclude with speeches from the two front benches. Ministers and their 'shadows' have other important privileges: by convention they are allowed to speak for far longer than back-benchers (usually for forty or so minutes when opening, and at least fifteen to twenty minutes when summing up), and their prominent positions behind the despatch boxes give them a significant debating advantage. In a typical debate, more than a third of the available time will be taken up by frontbenchers – and often more than that in short debates.

In most debates there is not enough time available for all those backbenchers wishing to speak to do so. In theory, MPs simply take their chance at 'catching the Speaker's eye' every time the floor is free; in fact, proceedings are rather less spontaneous than that: MPs hoping to speak in a debate usually notify the Speaker's office beforehand, and the Speaker weighs up claims – taking account of how often an MP has spoken before and his 'claims' to speak in a particular debate – before producing an informal 'batting order'. Members are called alternately from each side, with one Liberal Democrat MP called in most debates and generally also an MP from a minor party. In consequence, government back-benchers tend to get less than their 'fair share' of the floor – a cause of considerable frustration when the government has a large majority (as since 1983). A more general source of irritation is the custom of according Privy Councillors – for the most part former Cabinet ministers – priority in debates. As a partial remedy, the House has agreed to a ten-minute limit on speeches in the middle two hours of popular debates.

Impact of debate
Commons debates range widely. Here, for example, are the subjects debated in May 1989 (aside from issues raised on the adjournment):

2 May	Opposition day:	(1) NHS White Paper, doctors' response
		(2) Teacher shortages
11 May	Government motion: NHS White Paper	
12 May	Private member's motion: 'Active citizenship'	
15 May	Private member's motion: Transport	
16 May	Opposition day:	(1) Cost of government publicity
		(2) Manufacturing industry

18 May   Government motion: Developments in the European Community

19 May   Private member's motion: Domestic and satellite broadcasting

22 May   Spring adjournment debates

23 May   Opposition day: Inner cities

Yet despite their range and quantity, there is room for considerable scepticism as to the quality and impact of Commons debates. Most involve little more than ritual party-political point-scoring across the chamber with a higher premium on the trading of insults than the analysis of problems; for analysis and specialist knowledge Lords debates are markedly superior to those in the Commons. MPs show what they themselves think of debates by their habitual absence from them: once the frontbench speeches are over, it is rare to find more than half a dozen members scattered across the green benches, almost all of them present with a view to 'catching the Speaker's eye' in turn. Indeed, the word *debate* is something of a misnomer: little by way of challenging or responding to arguments actually takes place in a Commons 'debate'; rather, a succession of speeches are read into *Hansard*, with serious cut and thrust only during the frontbench speeches at the beginning and end, and then rarely with the intent of developing or probing the point at issue. Finally, in all but the most exceptional debate the vote is a foregone conclusion – so much so that it has long been the practice for the leading speakers to come on at the beginning, in time for the evening news bulletins, and not at the end before the division takes place.

Nonetheless, it would be a mistake to write off debates. Debates remain the prime means by which the Commons fulfils its 'expressive' function, and at times of crisis they can be used to express the national mood with devastating effect. Neville Chamberlain was forced to resign as wartime Prime Minister after two days of sustained criticism in the debate on the Norwegian campaign in May 1940. More recently, the 'mood' of the Commons weighed heavily in the days after the invasion of the Falkland Islands on 2 April 1982. In an emergency Saturday debate on the day after the invasion – broadcast live on radio and listened to by millions – Mrs Thatcher was left in no doubt that her political survival depended upon the expulsion of the Argentinian forces, by armed force if necessary. The Leader of the Opposition, Michael Foot, spelt out 'the rights and wrongs of this matter ... not only to the people in our country but to people throughout the world', and he swept the House with his peroration:

The government must now prove by deeds – they will never be able to do it by words – that they ... [will ensure] that foul and brutal aggression does not succeed in our world. If it does, there will be a danger not merely to the Falkland Islanders, but to people all over this dangerous planet.

The chairman of the 1922 Committee (of Tory backbenchers), who spoke next, declared that 'the Leader of the Opposition spoke for us all'. Two days later the entire team of Foreign Office ministers, headed by Lord Carrington, resigned and the 'task force' embarked for the South Atlantic.

On a more mundane level, whatever their limitations as means of considering and influencing policy, debates compel ministers continually and publicly to explain and justify their actions. And those who fail to do so convincingly will have a short ministerial life, whatever their other qualities. To take just recent cases, the dismissal of Paul Channon and John Moore from the Cabinet in the first 1989 reshuffle was widely attributed to their consistently poor performances on the Treasury bench. Similarly, the public disagreements between Nigel Lawson and Mrs Thatcher's economics adviser (Professor Walters), which led to the Chancellor's dramatic resignation in October 1989, were exacerbated by pressure from the Commons. In a heated Opposition day debate on the economy Mr Lawson was repeatedly pressed on Walters's status; his discomfiture was evident, and two days later he resigned.

Conversely, political reputations can be made almost entirely on the basis of ability at the Despatch Box. This is particularly true of Opposition politicians, who have little other way of establishing themselves and impressing their parliamentary colleagues or the media. The post-1987 rise of Bryan Gould, Gordon Brown, Robin Cook, John Prescott, Jack Straw and Tony Blair – reflected in their showings in the annual elections to the Shadow Cabinet – owed much to their debating successes on the front bench.

Whether debating prowess should be a prerequisite for ministerial office is itself debatable. But it is no mean test of intellectual capacity and of the ability to *persuade* – the skill crucial above all others to the effective politician. Debates may, therefore, be of only limited value as instruments of deliberation, still less for their concrete influence on government policy. But they make and break political reputations, and they oblige ministers continually to rationalise and justify their conduct. Given the untrammelled power available to a government with a Commons majority, all means by which ministers are made publicly accountable for its exercise are to be prized.

Televising the Commons

Whatever their individual thirst for media attention, MPs collectively have always been wary of those seeking to broadcast their debates. Parliamentary reporting of any kind was banned until the late eighteenth century. Radio broadcasting was introduced only in 1978. And not until 1988 did the Commons finally succumb and vote to allow in the television cameras (egged on by the Lords who had been on TV since 1985). Televised transmission of the Commons began on 21 November 1989. Broadcasters were unhappy with the tight restrictions imposed – only the Member speaking can be shown, with other members and interruptions forbidden from being screened – but in practice the rules are not unduly restrictive.

'TV would erode the reputation of the House and permanently damage its traditional character', Mrs Thatcher said in opposing its introduction. (Following her lead Tory MPs voted 2:1 against the cameras, which triumphed only because of overwhelming support – 6:1 – from Labour.) In fact, most commentators agree that TV has made little impact on the Commons' traditional character – except perhaps marginally to improve it by notably reducing the level of heckling and barracking. On the other hand, the benefits are un-doubted. For the first time the Commons itself has taken centre stage in reporting from Westminster. And not only in news bulletins. The Commons has its own prime-time slot on BBC2, with a programme called *Westminster* put out at 8.15 p.m. every weekday evening (for fifteen minutes on Mondays and half an hour on Tuesdays to Fridays). BBC2 also runs a longer summary – *Westminster Week* – between 12 noon and 1 p.m. on Sundays, and gives live coverage to Prime Minister's Questions on Tuesdays and Thursdays. Channel Four has coverage on a similar basis. As for television's wider impact on public perceptions of politicians and Parliament, only time will tell.

7
Committees in the House of Commons

Without some division of labour, the House of Commons would be unable to legislate or scrutinise effectively, if at all. An assembly of 650 is not a suitable forum for undertaking the detailed business of revision and investigation, which can be better – or only – performed by smaller bodies with delegated authority from the House itself. For these and others reasons an elaborate committee structure has evolved in the Commons, which is explained and assessed in this chapter.

The principal types of Commons committee are:

Standing committees. It will be recalled from Chapter 5 that all public bills are subjected to line-by-line scrutiny after their principle has been endorsed on second reading. Most bills undergo their 'committee stage' in a *standing committee* established specifically for the purpose ('standing' because a number of such committees used to be set up for the whole of each session, though now it is usual to appoint a separate one for each bill).

Select committees. A select committee is simply a committee 'selected' from the House and charged to work according to specific terms of reference agreed by the House. For the most part, however, they are appointed for the purpose of scrutinising the policies and administration of the executive.

The most important committee work of the Commons is conducted by standing and select committees, and they will be examined further below. There are, however, several other types of committee, of which the following are particularly notable:

Joint committees. These are select committees composed of members of both the House of Commons and House of Lords meeting as one committee, and are the only formal forums in which members of both Houses can deliberate together. There is one 'standing' joint committee, concerned with the scrutiny of Statutory Instruments (see Chapter 5), but each session others are set up on an *ad hoc* basis.

Party committees. Each of the political parties in the Commons has a network of committees for its own MPs. Strictly speaking, these are not part of the committee system of the House itself, but they are so integral to its work that they ought properly to be considered as such. The main party committees are the Conservative *1922 Committee* – which includes all Tory backbenchers – and the *Parliamentary Labour Party* – which includes all Labour MPs, frontbenchers and back-benchers. Both have their own chairmen and officers, and the 1922 also has an executive committee; both also have numerous sub-committees (see Chapter 2).

Committees of the Whole House. Sometimes the entire House meets as a committee to conduct the committee stage of a bill. When this happens the House calls itself a 'Committee of the Whole House', and is presided over by a chairman, not the Speaker. Committees of the Whole House are used routinely only for part of the committee stage of the annual Finance Bill. But by convention the committee stages of bills of major constitutional significance (like the Scottish and Welsh devolution legislation of 1978) are taken at least in part by committees of the Whole House.

Grand Committees. Four or five times a session all MPs from Scotland and Wales meet as the Scottish Grand Committee and Welsh Grand Committee respectively. Meetings are usually held in London, but the Scottish Grand Committee sits in Edinburgh from time to time. The Grand Committees debate legislation and other matters affecting Scotland and Wales, but though they can pass motions they cannot bind the House of Commons itself. Since the Conservatives currently hold only ten of Scotland's seventy-two seats, and eight of the thirty-eight in Wales, it is not difficult to see the problems arising for the government if they could.

'Domestic' committees. These are responsible for the Commons' domestic arrangements, the most important of them being the *Procedure Committee* which considers and reports on possible changes to the committees, procedure and business arrangements of the House.

Standing committees

Standing committees are set up principally for the purpose of scrutinising bills at their committee stage. The Commons set up its first standing committees in 1878 and formalised the arrangement in 1882. They have been in use continuously since then, but their number has steadily increased – and since at least 1918 they have formed an integral part of the legislative machinery of the House. Standing committees today tend to have fewer members than in the past: the two standing committees set up in 1882 had between sixty and eighty members each; by 1919 the number of committees had risen to six and the membership reduced to forty; since the 1940s up to ten committees have been set up each session, with about twenty-five members apiece (though committees can, and still occasionally do, have up to fifty members).

Though most standing committees are set up to consider bills, some – like the six standing committees charged with considering Statutory Instruments – have other functions.

Procedure

Every bill is referred to a standing committee after its second reading unless the House directs otherwise. At any one time up to eight government bills will be in standing committees (tagged 'A' to 'H').

Standing committees are composed of MPs appointed by the *Committee of Selection*, which appoints on the nomination of the party whips, ensuring that committees reflect the party balance of the House itself. One or more ministers from the relevant department, and their Opposition 'shadows', are automatically appointed to each committee. Chairmen are selected by the Speaker from the *Chairmen's Panel*, a group of about twenty senior backbenchers from both sides of the House.

Standing committees consider amendments tabled to bills line by line and clause by clause. In contrast to select committees, they have no power to take evidence or interrogate witnesses;* their deliberations

* Apart from *special standing committees*, for which see p. 174.

consist solely in the consideration of amendments moved by committee members. Standing committee chairmen have wide-ranging powers (to select amendments, etc.) which they can use to expedite business; even so, if ministers believe that a bill is moving through a committee too slowly, they can move a guillotine motion on the floor of the House (see p. 70). When a bill has completed its passage through a standing committee it is 'reported' to the full House, at which stage further amendments can be moved on the floor of the House before the bill proceeds to third reading.

Impact

Standing committees are microcosms of the House itself, complete with front and back benches, whips and division bells. And the resemblance is more than simply a matter of form: party discipline operates in the same way in standing committees as on the floor of the House. A government with a small majority (or no majority at all) will be vulnerable to defeat in standing committees: the 1974–79 Labour government suffered more than a hundred standing committee defeats, some of them involving notable changes to legislation (even to rates of taxation). But that was exceptional: all but two of the other post-war governments have commanded substantial Commons majorities and suffered no more than a handful of largely inconsequential defeats in standing committees. The great majority of amendments actually carried are moved by ministers, and only occasionally in response to committee debates.

What this means in practice can be seen by examining the standing committee scrutiny of the two most important government bills of the 1988/89 session: the legislation to privatise and restructure the electricity and water industries. The bills took thirty-six and thirty-five sittings respectively to pass through their standing committees, in both cases taking up well over 100 hours of deliberation spread over some ten weeks. Thirty-seven votes took place on amendments proposed to the Electricity Bill and forty-seven on amendments to the Water Bill, *not one* of them resulting in an amendment being made to either bill. In all, 114 amendments were made to the Electricity Bill: 113 were moved by ministers; Opposition MPs moved 227, not one of which was carried; Conservative backbenchers moved twenty-two, one of which was accepted by the government (without a vote), one defeated and the rest withdrawn. At the end of 110 hours of consideration, therefore, no amendment moved by the government had been rejected and only one minor amendment moved by an MP other than a minister had been agreed to.

However, it was the Water Bill which showed the standing committees at their most absurd. Twenty-seven hours were spent discussing the bill's first clause and after a total of seventy-five hours of debate the committee had reached only clause 9 – out of the bill's 180. At that rate of progress it would have taken the committee eighty weeks – and about 1,400 hours – to have completed its deliberations; so the government resorted to a guillotine motion to limit consideration of the remaining 171 clauses to a further month (i.e. about another seventy-eight hours of debate). In all, therefore, the bill took more than 150 hours to pass through committee, virtually all of it spent debating amendments which ministers never had any intention of meeting with other than a blank refusal. Ritual run riot?

Select committees before 1979

The select committee structure of the House of Commons was overhauled in 1979, with consequences explained below. However, two of the more important select committees in existence pre-date the reforms:

* The *Public Accounts Committee*, set up more than a century ago, is charged with 'the examination of the accounts showing the appropriation of the sums granted by Parliament to meet the public expenditure, and of such other accounts laid before Parliament as the Committee may think fit'. It forms a vital part of the Commons' machinery for scrutinising the government's use of public funds, and will be considered further in Chapter 8.

* The *Parliamentary Commissioner for Administration* (or *'Ombudsman') Committee* is a nine-member committee established in 1967 to supervise the work of the newly-created Parliamentary Commissioner for Administration (known as the 'Ombudsman'). The Ombudsman's job is to investigate complaints of maladministration levelled against central government departments, public agencies and the National Health Service. The Ombudsman – currently Sir Anthony Barrowclough QC – is a government appointee, but since 1977 the chairman of the Ombudsman Committee has been consulted about the appointment. Only MPs can refer cases to the Ombudsman, and in all some 800 complaints are considered by him (with the assistance of some ninety staff) each year, of which about 100 are held to be at least partially justified. The committee's role is to survey and comment

on the Ombudsman's activities; it does so in two or three reports each session.

Numerous other select committees existed before 1979, with responsibility for examining areas such as nationalised industries, science and technology policy, overseas development, race relations and European legislation. But by the mid-1970s MPs were expressing growing concern about the essentially *ad hoc*, almost random nature of their activities. This concern culminated, in 1976, in a commission to the Procedure Committee to consider how the Commons could be made 'more effective [in the] performance of its functions'. The Procedure Committee's report, published in 1978, recommended the wholesale replacement of most of the existing select committee structure with a new system of committees to provide systematic scrutiny of the work of each government department. The committee's motives were clearly stated:

The House should no longer rest content with an incomplete and unsystematic scrutiny of the activities of the Executive merely as a result of historical accident or sporadic pressures, and it is equally desirable for the different branches of the public service to be subject to an even and regular incidence of select committee investigation into their activities and to have a clear understanding of the division of responsibilities between the committees which conduct it.

The committee insisted that its proposals represented 'changes in practice of an evolutionary kind, following naturally from present practices'. But its report was controversial nevertheless. The Labour government of the day was not enthusiastic at the prospect of 'watchdogs with teeth', and Michael Foot, then Labour's deputy leader and Leader of the House of Commons, was strongly opposed to the new committees, fearing they would detract from the floor of the House ('the supreme attribution of the House of Commons which distinguishes it and makes the place that it ought to be'). However, the Tory Opposition supported the proposals – largely because it *was* the Opposition – and so did most backbenchers; even Enoch Powell, usually an arch conservative on procedural matters, gave them his blessing. 'They will', he argued, 'simply be doing more thoroughly, more consistently, but in much the same way, the work which the Select Committees ... have hitherto found themselves led into doing.' Fortuitously, the report was published just before a change of government and Norman St John Stevas, Mrs Thatcher's first Leader of the Commons, welcomed the Procedure Committee's proposals as 'a necessary preliminary to the effective scrutiny of government'. By all accounts, Tory enthusiasm for the watchdogs waned after the party's election victory; but St John Stevas moved swiftly and the new select committee structure was inaugurated in June 1979.

Departmental select committees

Structure and composition

There are currently thirteen departmental select committees (DSCs). They shadow the work of every department except the Lord Chancellor's and the Scottish Office,* with freedom to range beyond their strict departmental boundaries if necessary.

The DSCs each have eleven members, all of them backbenchers – i.e. no ministers, parliamentary private secretaries or Opposition front-bench spokesmen serve on them. Turnover of members is low: an average of less than 15% per annum. Only one committee (Treasury and Civil Service) at present has a sub-committee.

The party balance on DSCs reflects that of the House itself. In October 1987 a total of 143 MPs had places. Of those, 83 (58%) were Conservatives, 52 (36%) Labour, 4 (3%) SDP/Liberal and 4 (3%) from the minor parties. Committee chairmanships were divided between the two major parties – another feature peculiar to the DSCs** – in the ratio of 9 Conservative to 4 Labour in 1987. Chairmen are for the most part senior backbenchers (see Table 7.1) elected to serve for an entire parliament and sometimes more than one (Sir Ian Lloyd, chairman of the Energy Committee continuously since 1979, holds the record). More than two-thirds of the current chairmen have never held government office; only one (David Howell, chairman of the Foreign Affairs Committee) is a former Cabinet minister. Sir Ian Lloyd is a typical figure: a south coast MP since 1964 who has never held office but was a long-time member of the science and technology committee and founder and first chairman of the all-party committee on information technology; in addition to the Energy Committee he also chairs the Conservative backbench shipping and shipbuilding subcommittee – in

---

* The Scottish Affairs Committee has not been set up since the 1987 election because of the shortage of Tory backbenchers from Scotland willing to serve, making it impossible to compose the committee with a Tory majority.
** With one exception: the Public Accounts Committee is traditionally chaired by a senior Opposition Member.

Table 7.1 Chairmen of departmental select committees, 1988

Committee	Chairman	Party	Chmn since	MP since	Former minister?
Agriculture	Jerry Wiggin	Con	1987	1969	Yes
Defence	Michael Mates	Con	1987	1974	No
Education	Timothy Raison	Con	1987	1970	Yes
Employment	Ron Leighton	Lab	1983	1979	No
Energy	Sir Ian Lloyd	Con	1979	1964	No
Environment	Sir Hugh Rossi	Con	1983	1966	Yes
Foreign Affairs	David Howell	Con	1987	1966	Yes
Home Affairs	John Wheeler	Con	1987	1979	No
Social Services	Frank Field	Lab	1987	1979	No
Trade & Industry	Kenneth Warren	Con	1983	1970	No
Transport	David Marshall	Lab	1987	1979	No
Treasury & Civil Service	Terence Higgins	Con	1983	1964	Yes
Welsh Affairs	Gareth Wardell	Lab	1983	1982	No

short, a House of Commons man *par excellence*, but virtually unknown beyond the committee corridor.

The *Liaison Committee*, comprising the chairmen of all the DSCs, presides over the DSC structure and is responsible for ensuring its smooth running of the structure and 'general matters relating to [committees'] work'.

Procedure and activities

The select committees are appointed 'to examine the expenditure, administration and policy of the principal government departments ... and associated public bodies'. They do so by means of investigations leading to published reports. Most committees publish one or two major reports each session, along with a number of reports on more minor issue. The precise topics of the reports are selected by the committees themselves at the start of each session. The Energy Committee, for example, published six reports in the 1985/6 session, two of them major (on the regulation of the privatised gas industry and on combined heat and power), three of more modest proportions (on mining subsidence, crude oil prices and the Department of Energy's spending plans), and one responding to the government's own response to an earlier report.

The committees have a numerous powers and means of assistance at their disposal in the task of gathering evidence and preparing reports:

* *Written memoranda*. Committees have the power to send for 'persons, papers and records' when gathering evidence. They solicit written evidence from government departments, public bodies, pressure groups, academics and other interested parties.

* *Examination of witnesses*. Each committee spends a majority of its time interviewing witnesses – notably ministers, senior civil servants and individuals and groups who have submitted memoranda. With the support of the House itself the committees can compel attendance, but it has not yet proved necessary to do so.

* *Visits*. Committees can make official visits at home and abroad as part of their work. During the 1987/8 session they paid a total of twenty-two visits abroad and sixty-one to locations within the UK.

* *Specialist advisers and researchers*. Each committee is advised by specialists in its area, who work for it on a part-time basis (in some cases advising a committee over a period of years). In 1987/8 a total of seventy-five specialist advisers were employed. Most committees also have at least one full-time researcher.

* *Clerks of the House*. Each committee is assisted by at least one clerk with support staff.

Table 7.2 gives statistics relating to the work of the select committees in the 1987/8 session.

Impact

Over the past ten years DSCs have made a distinct contribution to the work of the Commons, but they have not had the effect that their proponents hoped or that their opponents feared. For all their work, the Commons still remains essentially chamber-oriented; and the scrutiny and investigative work of the committees has, for the most part, made little noticeable impact on government policy.

The most frequently alleged shortcomings of the select committees are fourfold:

* *Inadequate resources*. The DSCs operate with minimal support staff and on a shoestring budget. The total number of clerks, assistants and secretaries employed to service the entire DSC structure in 1987/8 was fifty-nine – about the number employed to staff *one* typical

Table 7.2 Select committees, 1987/8 session

Committee	Members	Former ministers	Party of chairman	Attendance record of members (%)	Meetings	Reports	Witnesses Civil servants	Ministers	Others	Special advisers	Committee votes	Sessional costs (£000)
Agriculture	11	0	Con	68	24	5	30	3	66	3	0	24
Defence	11	1	Con	76	33	12	24	2	17	13	0	40
Education	11	1	Con	75	30	3	21	2	85	5	0	21
Employment	11	1	Lab	76	36	4	19	2	79	4	0	28
Energy	11	0	Con	75	33	8	9	3	70	7	4	16
Environment	11	1	Con	73	28	7	15	1	54	4	0	32
Foreign Affairs	11	4#	Con	81	46	4	23	4	30	6	5	22
Home Affairs	11	0	Con	73	28	7	21	1	47	0	0	11
Scotland	–	–	–	–	–	–	–	–	–	–	–	–
Social Services	11	1	Lab	81	29	7	22	4	42	11	0	18
Trade & Industry	11	2	Con	75	40	4	18	4	96	3	0	61
Transport	11	0	Lab	69	33	5	26	1	72	7	0	49
Treasury & Civil Service*	11	0	Con**	73	43	12	41	5	26	9	3	17
Welsh Affairs	11	1	Lab	76	20	3	7	1	40	6	0	16

Notes: * Including one (Civil Service) sub-committee.

     ** Labour chairman of sub-committee.

     # Including two former Cabinet ministers, one of them (David Howell) the chairman.

standing committee of the US Congress and far fewer than the committee staff of any other west European legislature.* Each DSC operates with around half a dozen full-time officials and a similar number of professional advisers. The total expense of servicing all the select committees in 1987/8 was around £1.2 million − which, to give some idea of proportion, might be compared with the roughly £61 million spent by the armed services on military bands alone in the same year. Moreover, committees are heavily reliant on the government itself for evidence, and almost totally so for financial information: the Commons has nothing to compare with the powerful Congressional research agencies which provide invaluable facilities for Congressional committees.

Such minimal resources severely restrict the volume and depth of the DSCs' activities. Most committees are capable of producing only one or two major reports a session: DSC scrutiny has a distinctly random quality about it, with major aspects of the work of departments never being investigated.

* *Limitations on the scope of investigations.* It is generally thought that the DSCs pay too little attention to issues of expenditure and financial management within their departments. Furthermore, they cannot consider legislation; a central aspect of the work of government is thus completely beyond their competence. However, in practice committees have sought to circumvent this restriction by examining matters likely to lead to legislation in the near future. In 1988, for example, the Energy Committee produced a detailed report on the structure, regulation and economic consequences of electricity privatisation − four months before the government introduced its bill to privatise the electricity supply industry. But such initiatives have been exceptional, and have anyway taken place too late to make any noticeable difference to the shape of legislation.

* *Ministerial disregard of reports.* The government is obliged to publish a response to every report by a DSC. But only a handful of reports since 1979, and those on matters of low political salience (like the Home Affairs Committee report on the 'stop and search' laws) have made any appreciable impact on policy. For the most part the reports are ignored − or, if critical of ministers, treated with contempt.

---

* Even so, Commons committees are not necessarily less effective in consequence. The French National Assembly, for example, has only six scrutiny committees, four of sixty-one members and two with more than 100 members.

In the summer of 1989 a widely previewed report of the Health and Social Services Committee critical of the government's Health Service reforms was rubbished by ministers before it had even been published. And once reports have been published, committees have few means of creating momentum behind them. Reports have the status of recommendations to the House, but the Commons itself largely ignores the work of its committees: only a handful of reports are debated on the floor of the House and not many more are given other than cursory attention by the media. Furthermore, select committee chairmen are, with only rare exceptions, figures unknown to the media and wider public – which makes the task of catching the headlines all the more difficult.

   * *Mistaken role.* Select committees tend to work on a consensual rather than conflictual basis, and most of their members strive hard to overcome party divisions and produce unanimous reports. In their early years it was often alleged that, in consequence, their investigations and reports were anodyne, if not bordering on the petty. Consensus, wrote Gavin Drewry in his lengthy 1985 study of the DSCs, was secured 'at the high price of excessive blandness and marginality as committees cast around for subjects that will not be too divisive'. Since 1985, however, the DSCs – or most of them – have moved rapidly in the other direction, tackling head-on issues of central party political controversy like privatisation, the trade-union ban at GCHQ, the Westland affair and the future of the NHS. Investigations of this kind have sometimes strained the cohesion and consensual practices of the committees, in at least one case to breaking point;* though for the most part they have held together even when dealing with controversial matters. But this shift in emphasis has, in turn, attracted sharp criticism from observers like George Jones, who believe the committees should concentrate on *administration*, not *policy*. 'It is illogical', George Jones argues,

to have one group of the most senior parliamentarians setting policy ... and another group of only nine to eleven MPs (in practice usually fewer), harassing the government and expecting to be recognised as authoritative. The role of

---

* Heated controversy within the Education Committee on a series of controversial investigations led Timothy Raison to resign the chairmanship in October 1989. It was reported that 'His sudden resignation, during an acrimonious private meeting, followed bitter disputes between Labour and Tory members over politically sensitive committee reports.'

the House of Commons is not to be a counter-government, but an arena for contending views, above all between government and opposition.

Put like this, the argument has force. But it too readily assumes that the role of the committees *is* to set 'rival' policies. Certainly, DSCs often recommend that ministers consider alternative courses of action – something which non-ministerial MPs, whether on the government's own backbenches or the Opposition side, do all the time. Yet that is only one aspect, and arguably one of the less important, of the committees' role. For it is the *processes* of the select committees – the taking of written and oral evidence, examination of ministers and civil servants, review of departmental procedures – which are their most valuable features, serving as they do to strengthen the Commons' scope for scrutiny and making Parliament more accessible to those affected by, and with views on, policy issues. Reports are only one 'output' of the DSCs, and it is unclear how these features could be fully preserved if the committees were restricted to 'administration', however that might be defined. Moreover, in becoming more effective a *scrutineer*, there is no evidence that the Commons has become any less effective an *arena* – indeed, if anything the 'contending views between government and opposition' will come over even more sharply on TV than before, regardless of work done on the committee corridor.

The last section has touched on the beneficial effects of select committees. Three stand out in particular:

* *Professionalism of MPs.* The DSCs have played a part in giving MPs who want to be full-timers a full-time job to do, and in providing them with more than superficial knowledge of at least one branch of governmental activity. About one in three of all MPs not on one of the front benches, or a PPS, now serves on a select committees.

* *Profile and reputation of the Commons.* The DSCs have undoubtedly enhanced the profile and reputation of the House of Commons among policy-formers and the media, though they have still to make an impression on the wider 'informed public'. Furthermore, they have notably increased access to Parliament for pressure groups and other interested parties. This has, on occasion, been highlighted to dramatic effect – for example with the Foreign Affairs Committee's 1989 investigation into the nationality status of British subjects in Hong Kong, which fortuitously took place at the same time as the suppression of the pro-democracy movement in China. At the height of the crisis, the Foreign Secretary and the Governor of Hong Kong spent a morning

each being cross-examined by the committee, the Governor using it as a forum to publicise his advice urging ministers to extend British citizenship rights to Hong Kong subjects. Nothing better demonstrated the select committees' ability to strengthen the Commons in its performance of its *expressive* role, and thereby to give MPs a distinctly larger, if indeterminate, influence on the decision-making process.

* *Scrutiny of the Executive.* The scrutiny provided by the DSCs is at best uneven, but it represents a vast improvement on the pre-1979 *régime*. Moreover, in so far as the investigative arm of a legislature is intended to curb maladministration or worse, it depends for its efficacy as much upon what ministers and civil servants believe it *might* reach as upon the actual extent of its grasp year by year. Both the committees' actual grasp, and its potential reach, have extended considerably as a result of the 1979 reforms, and ministers and civil servants − both now used to accounting for themselves before committees as never before − are well aware of the fact.

'Chinese walls'

At a deeper level, perhaps the most significant impact of the departmental select committees lies not so much in the specific improvements wrought by them as in the 'Chinese Walls' they have erected within the Commons itself. For the DSCs have engineered a partial but distinct institutional separation between the Commons' machinery for executive scrutiny on the one hand, and its forums for legislative and party political business on the other. The arenas for the latter are the chamber and standing committees (the last essentially microcosms of the chamber), both alike battlegrounds in which the last and next general elections are perpetually fought.

Departmental select committees are not worlds apart. The governing party has a majority on each committee, and MPs do not mysteriously shed their party colours on entering the committee corridor. But the select committees' modes of operation are fundamentally different from those pertaining in the other forums of the House. In the first place, neither whips nor frontbenchers are members of the DSCs: when a minister appears before one, he comes as witness not master. Secondly, the institutional separation is as much behavioural as procedural. Because of their size, composition and remit, DSCs place a premium on consensus, not division; on the rational formulation of policy, not the unthinking acceptance of party whips; on bipartisan scrutiny of ministerial and administrative actions, not the knee-jerk reflexes of government and Opposition. Select committees strive to work harmoniously and to agree reports unanimously, and their chairmen endeavour to avoid votes – still more minority reports – for fear of weakening their impact.

The behavioural distinctiveness of select committees is therefore essentially a matter of *situation*. For an MP is in a fundamentally different situation in a select committee to that which he occupies in his other roles. For once he is actually obliged to apply his own judgement to an issue, after exhaustive research and scrutiny. In doing so he is not simply free from formal party direction; he is subject to the pressure of *committee* loyalties, with inertia and undecided opinions – qualities exhibited by MPs on select committees as much as elsewhere – pulling an MP towards the committee consensus, not (as elsewhere in the House) towards the party line. Sometimes issues cut too sharply between parties for these forces to apply; but even then, the behavioural traits identified only fully cease to apply when it comes to drafting and agreeing a report.

The strength and resilience of the Chinese Walls should not be overstated. The 1978 Procedure Committee hoped that measures like the payment of select committee chairmen would help 'provide some element of a career opportunity in the House not wholly in the gift of the party Leaders'. Yet chairmen are not paid, and the DSC structure has failed to provide anything akin to an alternative Commons hierarchy. The committees in any case operate within too narrow a scope, and with too limited resources, to have had any transformative impact on the relationship between MPs and parties or Parliament and government. Nonetheless, the DSCs represent a definite institutional evolution, and it is not difficult to envisage extensions to the Chinese Walls which could give them an enhanced standing. It is significant that MPs themselves rate the committees highly: a 1989 MORI poll showed that more than three-quarters (77%) of Members surveyed considered select committees to be 'effective' at scrutinising the work of government – compared with only 49% who believed the traditional techniques of questions and debates to be so. 'In a real sense', as Professor Walkland has written, 'the committees represent a new House-of-Commons-in-waiting. How long it will have to wait I don't know.'

8

The House of Commons and finance

The raising and controlling of government spending lie at the very heart of the Commons' *raison d'être*. Medieval monarchs first summoned Parliament because they needed to raise money – usually to fight wars – and sought to induce representatives of the nation's wealthy to agree to new or heavier taxes. For centuries after, the levying of taxation and the uses to which royal revenue was put were perennial sources of conflict between Crown and Commons – indeed, the seventeenth-century Civil War grew out of Parliament's refusal to vote Charles I 'aids and supplies', and the King's attempt to levy taxes (including the notorious 'Ship Money') without recourse to Parliament. After the Restoration financial relations became somewhat less fraught, largely because successive eighteenth-century monarchs and their ministers followed policies broadly acceptable to the Commons. Even so, until the massive post-Victorian expansion in central government spending, MPs continued jealously to guard their control of the purse strings.

In the twentieth century, however, things have been very different, for two main reasons:

* *Rise in public spending.* Until 1914 government spending never represented more than 10% of national income. Since then it has risen sharply, especially since the Second World War, with the creation of the 'Welfare State' and a massive extension of governmental activity elsewhere. Public expenditure for the financial year 1988/9 was projected at £153 billion, two-thirds of which was due to be spent on just five sectors: social security (£25 billion), health (£23 billion), defence (£20 billion), education and science (£20 billion) and police and prisons (£7 billion). This marked a slight – relative – reduction on the spending levels of ten years previously, but still represented some

40% of all national income, or £3,000 for every man, woman and child in Britain.

* *Subservient Commons*. As we have seen, the Commons by and large does the bidding of Her Majesty's Government; and that applies as much to the raising and spending of public money as to everything else. Parliament no longer regards itself as bound to limit spending and restrain taxation *per se*; its decisions on fiscal issues, like others, are determined by the political priorities of the party in power.

Despite these fundamental changes, Parliament's procedures for dealing with financial matters are still largely the product of past practices and assumptions. Pre-eminent among them is the convention that Ministers of the Crown, and they alone, may *initiate* requests for funds, while the role of the Commons is to *grant* (or refuse to grant) such requests and to *control* the expenditure of money once voted. Thus the Commons does not vote money at all unless requested to do so by the government; nor does it impose taxes unless ministers deem them to be necessary for the public service. And the Lords plays no part in the process: its one attempt to meddle in financial matters at the turn of the century was ill-fated and has not been repeated.

This chapter surveys the processes of initiation, granting and control which make up the Commons' financial procedure. By way of introduction, we start with the Commons' financial year, and from there proceed to examine the principal mechanisms of Commons' financial control.

Table 8.1 sets out the principal events in the Commons' financial year; the content and significance of them are explained below.

Taking these annual events one by one:

The autumn statement. Sir Geoffrey Howe's 1982 autumn statement was the first of its kind, but his successors (Nigel Lawson and John Major) have continued the practice and it has become an established feature, usually occurring in early November. In thirty or so pages, the statement sets out the Treasury's view of the general state of the economy and the prospects for government revenue over the coming year; it also discloses the government's projected ceiling for public spending (i.e. all spending by public bodies, including local authorities) for the coming financial year, a figure essential to numerous subsequent announcements on spending levels (uprating of benefits, size of local government grants, etc.). The Commons Treasury and Civil Service Committee (TCSC) immediately sets about an enquiry into the

Table 8.1 The Commons' financial year

Date	Information and estimates presented to the Commons, etc.	Voting timetable
November to February	(1) Autumn financial statement (2) Winter supplementary estimates (3) Votes on account (4) Consolidated Fund Bill	Voted on not later than 6 February
January to March	(5) Public Expenditure White Paper (6) Main estimates (7) Spring supplementary estimates (8) Excess votes (9) Consolidated Fund Bill (10) Budget statement (11) Finance Bill	Items 7 & 8 voted on not later than 18 March; bills (9, 11, 13) enacted March–July
April to August	(12) Summer supplementary estimates (extra sums needed for current year) (13) Consolidated Fund (Appropriation) Bill	Voted on not later than 5 August

statement; its report, along with the White Paper itself, form the basis of a Commons debate shortly before Christmas.

The Public Expenditure White Paper, published in late January or early February, is a more detailed statement – running to some nineteen volumes in 1989 – which breaks down the total in the Chancellor's autumn statement into figures for each department. Like the autumn statement, the White Paper forms the subject of an enquiry by the TCSC; and the White Paper and report are subject to a Commons debate – opened by the Chief Secretary, who has immediate responsibility for public spending – in mid-February.

However, an important change to the arrangement above is imminent. Taking up recommendations of the TCSC made in 1987, the government intends to replace the Public Expenditure White Paper with an expanded autumn statement accompanied by a series of departmental papers — the latter to be both annual departmental reports to Parliament and detailed statements of forward spending plans.

The estimates give the government's detailed breakdown of expenditure department by department, and are the formal basis for the granting of money by the Commons. Until the late nineteenth century each estimate was debated and voted upon separately, thereby allowing almost any aspect of government policy to be debated on the floor of the House. Today only a few estimates are actually debated, the rest being approved formally. A number of different types of estimates are published and voted on during the course of the year, variously relating to the previous, current and subsequent year's spending. In consequence, the actual authorisation of supply expenditure for a given financial year extends over some 2½ years. About 45% of any one year's estimates are in fact voted on in advance ('votes on account'), and 'excess votes' are presented about eleven months after the end of the financial year to which they refer.

It is important to note that only *supply* expenditure — money spent (or to be spent) by or under the responsibility of a government department — is actually voted by the Commons. This constitutes some 70% of total public spending: the remainder is spent by other bodies, notably local authorities and the European Community, which have tax raising powers of their own, originally granted by Parliament but exercised without reference to it.

Consolidated Fund (CF) Bills. When the three main sets of supply estimates have been approved, Consolidated Fund Bills are introduced to give legal authorisation to the necessary expenditure. The 'Consolidated Fund' is simply the Exchequer account into which taxes and other government revenues are paid and from which most central government expenditure is made. Money voted to, but not spent by, departments in one financial year must be returned to the CF and cannot be carried over to the following year. There is also a *Contingency Fund* of up to 2% of the previous year's total expenditure for use in an emergency. CF bills have to pass through Parliament like other legislation; but debates on them have almost nothing to do with the Consolidated Fund: they are now the preserve of backbenchers who use the time allocated to raise any matters they wish, while the proceedings on the CF bills themselves are purely formal.

Budget statement. The Chancellor of the Exchequer's annual Budget statement has long been one of the great theatrical occasions of the parliamentary year. The Commons chamber is always packed to capacity, and even before the arrival of television the Chancellor's speech was invariably broadcast live on radio. It is now a rather briefer affair than of old. Gladstone's most famous Budget speech lasted nearly five hours, while Lloyd George managed four-and-a-half with his famous 'People's Budget' of 1909. A more restrained sixty to seventy minutes is the norm today. When the Chancellor has sat down, the Leader of the Opposition immediately responds, and a four day debate on the Budget ensues.

In his speech the Chancellor surveys the state of the economy and public revenue and announces changes he proposes to make to taxes and other duties. In fact, the oral statement is only a summary version of a much longer and more detailed financial report published at the same time; and though some of the Chancellor's budgetary proposals (like changes to tax rates on petrol and alcohol) take immediate effect through financial resolutions passed by the Commons within hours of the speech, most of the proposals have to go through a lengthy process of parliamentary scrutiny before they become law.

The *Finance Bill* is the vehicle for passing the Budget's provisions into law. It goes through the same stages as any other public bill, except that its committee stage is divided into two: the more important clauses (relating to tax changes) are customarily taken on the floor of the House, while the rest of the bill goes to a standing committee. It is highly unusual for the Commons to alter the Budget in any other than trifling respects: the experience of the minority Labour government of 1976–79, which suffered a number of defeats on its Finance Bills (including an amendment to the 1978 Budget reducing the basic rate of income tax) was quite exceptional.

Commons' financial scrutiny

The stages in the Commons' financial year described above concern the government's initiation of financial proposals and the mechanisms through which the Commons grants (or refuses to grant) ministerial requests. But there is another side to the financial role of the Commons: control of the raising and spending of public money once voted.

Procedures for oversight and control

The Commons maintains an oversight of government spending in a number of ways.

1. *Debates*. As we have seen, every stage in the public expenditure cycle involves debate on the floor of the Commons. The debate on the Budget is second in length only to the annual debate on the Queen's Speech; the other statements or White Papers receive at least one day's debate each. Most debates ostensibly concern the government's proposals for future expenditure; but they are, naturally, heavily influenced by past practice.

So far as debates are concerned, the provision of oversight has improved somewhat in recent years. Before 1982 the days allocated for debates on the estimates (known as 'supply days') were given over to the Opposition to initiate debates of its own choosing; they had nothing whatever to do with the estimates as such. Since 1982, however, some twenty days have been designated 'Opposition days' (see p. 94), while four or so days each session have been set aside specifically for debates on the estimates, with the precise estimates to be debated selected by the *Liaison Committee* (see p. 107). This is still less than the eight days recommended for the purpose by a report of the Procedure Committee; but it at least ensures that the estimates are not passed entirely 'on the nod'.

2. *Legislation*. As we have seen, implementation of the government's financial proposals each year requires a number of bills, most of which must be debated and voted on like other legislation.

3. *Public Accounts Committee (PAC)*. The PAC is the cornerstone of the Commons' oversight structure. Established on Gladstone's initiative in 1860, it now consists of fifteen MPs chosen in proportion to party strength in the House, though by custom chaired by a senior member of the Opposition (often a former Treasury minister). The PAC is responsible for scrutinising the accounts of government departments and agencies to see that money is spent by those bodies on the specific matters for which it was voted. Its remit also includes 'economy, efficiency and effectiveness' studies, with the aim of ensuring that public money is spent to the maximum public advantage. 'The greatest thing about the committee's work', the PAC's current chairman (Robert Sheldon) told the Commons in December 1987:

is that its reports are unanimous. That is not to say that we have been emasculated in a party political sense. We remain politicians ... However, we also recognise that we cannot allow the taxpayer to get anything less than full value for the money that is spent on his behalf ... [But] it is not our duty to question the policies of the government and that is how we maintain our unanimity.

'Value for money' studies form an increasingly important part of the PAC's work. Where it finds abuse, its only effective recourse (provided those involved acted within the law) is to publicity; but that can be no mean sanction – as ministers and officials involved in the sale of Rover to British Aerospace in July 1988 found to their cost a year later when the National Audit Office (see below) published a report highly critical of the price and terms of the deal. Of the forty to fifty reports published in recent sessions – on issues as diverse as the De Lorean car project, falling school rolls and the measurement of farming incomes – about half have concerned the efficiency of expenditure; and it is the committee's intention that there should be fifty 'value for money' reports a year by 1992. Once a session the committee's reports are debated on the floor of the Commons, though most of the speakers in the invariably sparsely attended debate are themselves members of the PAC.

The PAC is by far the hardest working of the Commons' select committees, meeting twice a week for two to three hours a time during the session. However, crucial to its effectiveness is its back-up staff of auditors and investigators. These are provided by the *National Audit Office (NAO)*, established in its present form by the National Audit Act of 1983 with a staff of about 900 directed by the *Comptroller and Auditor General (CAG)*. The NAO has total financial and operational independence from the government: none of its staff are civil servants and the CAG (currently Mr John Bourn) is an officer of the House of Commons who reports directly to the PAC. The CAG has a considerable degree of autonomy: he decides – though with some input from the PAC – what departments and spheres of activity should be investigated by the NAO; and it is he who has formally to certify each department's *appropriation accounts* as being a valid record of the disbursement of funds voted by Parliament.

4. *Departmental select committees*. The remit of the departmental select committees – examined in detail in Chapter 7 – includes 'the expenditure ... of the principal government departments and associated bodies'. The *Treasury and Civil Service Committee (TCSC)* is

specifically responsible for Treasury and related matters: its current chairman is a former Treasury minister (Terence Higgins) and it is assisted by a sub-committee and by six part-time special advisers. In the 1987/8 session it published eight reports, most of them connected with the Autumn Statement, the Public Expenditure White Paper and the Budget.

5. *Question time*. Questions to Treasury ministers take place once a month during the session, and questions for written answer can be tabled at any time when the House is sitting (see Chapter 6).

How effective is Common oversight and control?

From the description above, the Commons might be thought to be equipped with an impressive range of instruments for ensuring adequate parliamentary control over the raising and spending of money. Yet in fact no aspect of its work is subject to more consistent and searching criticism. According to Sir Leo Pliatzky, a former Permanent Secretary to the Treasury, 'The formal procedures of the House for approving expenditure and taxation play virtually no substantive part in the decision making process.' And MPs themselves are dissatisfied with the system. The 1978 report of the Commons Procedure Committee was bitingly critial:

It is clear to us that the present financial procedures of the House are inadequate for ensuring control over public expenditure and ensuring that money is effectively spent. The House as a whole has long since ceased to exercise detailed control over public expenditure in any but the formal sense of voting the annual estimates and approving the Consolidated Fund and Appropriations Bills.

How justified are these criticisms today?

Defining the Commons' role

It is essential, at the outset, to define the role of MPs in matters of finance. This can best be done by addressing the most fundamental charge levied at the Commons – and implicit in the Procedure Committee's remarks – namely, that it almost never seeks to challenge the government's financial proposals. Is this true, and if so, is it a valid criticism?

In so far as ministerial defeats on financial matters are a rarity (minority governments excepted), it is indeed the case that the Commons almost never challenges the Chancellor's financial proposals.

But for it to do so in any but the most exceptional circumstances would totally undermine the existing relationship between government and Parliament. Responsible party government in Britain necessarily involves Parliament giving broad support to a government's policies – unless a majority are prepared to precipitate a general election. If a government were unable to secure majorities for its major financial proposals, its claim to the 'confidence' of the Commons would be threadbare.

The exigencies of parliamentary government apart, there is in any case good reason for doubting Parliament's ability to engage in the detailed business of economic policy-making. All MPs need to have at least an interest in economic and budgetary matters; but few have any expertise, and it is inconceivable that the Commons or its committees could, on an ongoing basis, exercise detailed control over the management of the economy. And the converse holds equally: in Britain it is ministers who have unambiguously to shoulder responsibility (in so far as any politicians do) for fiscal policy and economic failure. Parliamentary interference would inevitably result in the blurring, if not the destruction, of any clear locus of responsibility for economic management. The consequences of such a 'responsibility vacuum' are only too manifest in the United States, where a long-standing inability to tackle the serious federal budget deficit has been largely caused by the 'power' of Congress to avoid implementing electorally unpopular policies, combined with the ability of the President to avoid prime responsibility by blaming Congress for the *impasse*. The US also highlights another consequence of a system in which legislators are active participants in the process of budgetary decision-making: left to their own devices, most MPs would simply vote and lobby for spending policies to boost their re-election prospects.

It is by no means right, therefore, for the Commons to be blamed for failing to take financial decisions out of the hands of the Chancellor of the Exchequer and the Cabinet. That is not its proper role. Instead, concern should focus on the way in which the Commons performs those functions which undoubtedly pertain to it, namely oversight and control of the raising and spending of funds. And in these fields the Commons exhibits serious weaknesses, in two particular respects:

1. *Lack of professional assistance and information.* The ability to call on accurate information and to pursue taxpayers' money wherever it is spent is critical to the effectiveness of parliamentary financial control.

Yet the Commons' machinery for these purposes is far from adequate, though it is not as decrepit as it was even ten years ago, thanks to the National Audit Act. By creating the National Audit Office (NAO), giving it powers to carry out economy, efficiency and effectiveness audits, and by re-establishing the role of the Comptroller and Auditor-General (CAG) as an officer of the Commons, the act has at least ensured the existence of a professional scrutiny body detached from the Treasury and under no doubt as to its responsibilities. But the NAO is still severely constrained by a limited staff (despite its enormous brief it still has fewer than 900 employees, barely 10% more than the Exchequer and Audit Department which it replaced), and by a brief strictly confined to audit and value-for-money studies; large areas of public expenditure (like the nationalised industries) were excluded − at the government's insistence − from the NAO's remit when it was set up. Moreover, the NAO has no role comparable to that of the Congressional Budget Office for providing MPs with general economic and fiscal data independently of the Treasury. 'Knowledge is power'; yet for knowledge MPs are still largely dependent on those whom they are supposed to be scrutinising in the first place.

2. *Weakness of the Commons' scrutiny system.* Since the National Audit Act, however, the weakest link in the chain of parliamentary control has not been the lack of professional assistance and information, but the capacity of the Commons to do anything positive with it once provided. For the scrutiny machinery of the Commons, in so far as it involves MPs, remains hardly changed since the First World War. The Public Accounts Committee, assisted by the Comptroller and Auditor-General, strives valiantly to keep pace with the work entrusted to it. Yet public expenditure has, in real terms, increased more than tenfold over the past 120 years; while the Commons' system for scrutinising it has changed hardly at all since Gladstone set up the PAC and CAG 130 years ago. Even the modest increase in scrutiny provided by the NAO's value-for-money studies has proved too much for the PAC to manage. In a recent report on future plans, the PAC − which still operates without even *one* subcommittee − noted that 'the necessary work of the NAO in investigating the enormous field of public expenditure and taxation should not be limited by the capacity of this committee to take oral evidence, and that we [the PAC] should (as we have started

to do) exercise a measure of selection ...'. And this despite the fact that the CAG had warned the committee (as noted in the 1st report of 1986/7):

There are ... large fields of government activity which are extremely important and which on our present level of activity we are undoubtedly getting round to too slowly. It is not satisfactory that in major areas ... there are major activities in which we cannot expect to undertake any sort of study at all except on a cycle of eight years.

Yet if the PAC is clearly skimping on the work of financial scrutiny, the other Commons select committees hardly engage in it at all. One of the greatest weaknesses of the departmental select committees since 1979 has been their marked neglect of matters related to the estimates and financial administration of their departments. They are more easily attracted to issues of high political salience than the more humdrum, but no less important, matters contained in the Public Expenditure White Paper. And where spending has attracted their attention, it has tended to be supplementary estimates rather than the estimates themselves, since supplementary estimates often relate to *changes* in policy or the overshooting of original spending targets, which provide more political capital.

This weakness may, furthermore, come to be exacerbated by the government's proposed changes to civil service management structures. Acting on plans first mooted by Sir Robin Ibbs in his paper *The Next Steps*, the government has announced its intention to establish 'agencies' to carry out its executive functions in twenty-nine areas of activity employing some 170,000 civil servants in total. The Treasury and Civil Service Committee (8th report, 1987/8) has expressed its concern at the implications of the changes for parliamentary accountability. The TCSC wants the new agencies to be directly responsible to their relevant departmental select committee. But so far the government has stated only that the chief executives of the agencies will be designated as 'accounting officers' to Parliament, on much the same basis that permanent secretaries currently act for their departments, clearly intending that they should be substantially free from parliamentary scrutiny.

It is easy to see why Commons scrutiny of public revenue and expenditure leaves so much to be desired. There is little or no kudos available to the MP specialising in such matters; and even if there were, the degree of commitment, if not expertise, necessary to do the job effectively is too much for most of them. It may be, though, that if current trends continue, the National Audit Office and the Comptroller and Auditor-General will have developed a new form of 'remote control' oversight, whereby parliamentary scrutiny is conducted by Parliament's officers with little recourse to Parliament itself. It may not be satisfactory; but it is better than the alternative.

9
The House of Lords

The House of Lords, Britain's Second or Upper Chamber, has a fair claim to being the oldest legislative assembly in the world, unique – within representative democracies, at least – in its predominantly hereditary composition. Since the late fourteenth century the Lords has been a House of Parliament separate from the Commons, and its origins can be traced a few centuries further back. It has not been an unbroken history: Cromwell abolished the 'House of Peers' along with the Monarchy, declaring it to be 'useless and dangerous'. But the House of Lords reassembled at the Restoration in 1660, and has been an integral part of Parliament ever since.

Perhaps no institution exemplifies the adaptability of British institutions better than the House of Lords. Even the Monarchy, for all its remarkable status, has survived at the price of political impotence. The Lords, by contrast, has remained a hereditary and nominated assembly yet *retained* efficient functions. Admittedly, Bagehot consigned the peers of his day to the 'dignified' part of the constitution. Nowadays, however, the peers' decorous exhibitions hardly extend beyond providing a theatre for the State Opening of Parliament each year, an event that occupies all of sixty minutes. It is the business functions of the House which occupy the bulk of its time and effort.

But if the Lords is more than a quaint relic of bygone ages, its role in contemporary politics cannot be understood apart from its historical development. This chapter surveys the development of the composition, structure and powers of the Lords, with particular emphasis on changes this century. The following chapters will then look at the Lords at work and evaluate its contribution to Parliament today.

Composition of the Lords

The Lords can trace its roots back centuries before Parliament took
recognisable shape. The 'Great Council' summoned by medieval kings
(see Chapter 1) was gradually formalised as individual clerics and titled
aristocrats ('peers of the realm') established rights to a 'writ of
summons' to a House of Lords which sat separately from the Commons
in meetings of Parliament. All the while, though, the Lords remained
a small assembly. Indeed, the sixteenth-century Reformation of the
Church greatly reduced its size with a sharp decline in the number of
clerics. Not until the late eighteenth century did the Lords have more
than 200 members: it was large-scale peerage creation thereafter, by
Prime Ministers from Pitt the Younger to Lloyd George, which took
total membership to more than 700 by 1925.

Most members of the House of Lords are either hereditary peers
or life peers (see Table 9.1 for numbers). Hereditary peers are divided
into five ranks: duke, marquess, earl, viscount and baron, in descending
order of seniority. Life peers are all barons (or baronesses). But rank
confers no privileges in the proceedings of the House of Lords, nor
does any rank carry with it specific rights outside the Lords. To be more
precise about the two types of peerage:

Hereditary peers

An hereditary peer is an individual who has inherited a peerage by virtue
of his or her relationship to a deceased hereditary peer (a 'peer by
succession'), or one who has had an hereditary peerage conferred upon
him or her (a 'peer of first creation'). All peerages are created by the
Sovereign, now invariably on the advice of the Prime Minister of the
day. The rules governing the succession to peerages are complex and
not all hereditary peerages carry with them the right to a seat in the
House of Lords; but most do so, and almost all pass at death to male
heirs in the order of son, brother, uncle, nephew. If there is more than
one man in a category, age gives precedence – i.e. a title passes to the
eldest son of a deceased peer; if there are no sons to the eldest
brother, etc.

Few hereditary peerages have been created in recent years (none at
all between 1964 and 1983 and only four since Mrs Thatcher revived
the practice in 1983). Even so, peers who have succeeded to titles still
make up almost two-thirds of the Lords. The oldest extant title, the
barony de Ros, dates back as far as 1264; but only a small proportion

Table 9.1 Composition of the House of Lords (as at 31 August 1988)

Archbishops and bishops			26
Royal peers			5
Hereditary peers by succession:	dukes	24	
	marquesses	27	
	earls	151	
	viscounts	96	
	barons	439	
	baronesses	15	757
Hereditary peers of first creation:	earls	1	
	viscounts	7	
	barons	15	23
Life peers created under the Appellate Jurisdiction Act 1876 (law lords)			22
Life peers created under the Life Peerages Act 1958			354
			1187
Peers without writs of summons*			81
Peers on leave of absence**			177
			929

Notes: * Peers who are not entitled to seats in the Lords.
** Peers who have elected not to take any part in the proceedings of the Lords for the current Parliament.

of today's hereditary peers can trace their titles back centuries. The great majority of titles were created during the last 150 years, their first holders being for the most part politicians, great landowners or wealthy businessmen and industrialists.

The Queen does not belong to the House of Lords since she is herself a branch of Parliament. But the Prince of Wales is a member and four other members of the Royal Family possess hereditary peerages: the dukes of Edinburgh (Prince Philip), York (Prince Andrew), Gloucester and Kent. All five have taken their seats in the Upper House, though they never vote and only rarely attend or speak.

Peerages can be inherited at any age, but peers must be twenty-one before they can take their seats in the Lords. Since 1963 hereditary peers have been able to renounce their titles and with them membership of the Lords. Tony Benn and Lords Home and Hailsham took immediate advantage of this change in the law to disclaim their peerages and join or remain in the House of Commons (Sir Alec Douglas-Home, as he became, went on to serve as Prime Minister). But only twelve other peers have disclaimed, none since 1977. Hereditary peers do not often, in the main, attend the Lords; but they like to belong to the club – with free parking in central London!

Because of succession rules, almost all hereditary peers are men (though some ancient titles can be inherited by both men and women and the few women hereditary peers – twenty in 1989 – have been allowed to sit in the Lords since 1963). Unsurprisingly, hereditary peers come from diverse backgrounds. Many are still the heads of landed families with impeccable aristocratic credentials – perhaps somewhat irrelevant for a modern legislator, but not more so than those possessed by the third Lord Moynihan, who, according to Stuart Braham, used to play the bongos in a cabaret act with his former wife, a belly-dancer; or by the second Lord Teviot, an Etonian who was a slipper salesman in Harrods before spending six years as a bus driver (his conductress on the bus was Lady Teviot).

Life peers

Until 1958 women were not allowed to sit in the Upper House at all, and men – apart from a few senior judges (see below) – could only be made members by means of hereditary peerages giving seats in Parliament to their descendants in perpetuity. Why such remarkable restrictions remained unaltered for so long will be explained later; it needs simply to be noted here that Harold Macmillan's Conservative government (1957–63) sought to remove some of the more obvious anomalies without radically altering the composition of the Lords. It did this by the simple expedient of allowing peerages to be awarded for life only (i.e. incapable of being inherited) to both men and women. These reforms were enacted in the *Life Peerages Act* of 1958.

The Life Peerages Act has significantly changed the character of the Lords. More than 350 life peers, some fifty of them women, now have seats in the House, drawn from a much broader social, political and professional spectrum than the hereditary peerage. Most important of all, life peerages have been used by successive

Table 9.2 Peerage creations by Prime Ministers since 1958, by party

	Con	Lab	Lib/ SDP	Ind.	Total	Annual average
Macmillan/Home						
1958–64	17 (25)	29	1 (1)	18 (22)	65 (48)	17
Wilson						
1964–70	11	78	6	46	141	25
Heath						
1970–74	23	5	3	15	46	13
Wilson/Callaghan						
1974–79	17	82	6	34	139	27
Thatcher						
1979–89	78 (2)	38	9	37 (2)	162 (4)	16
Total	146	232	25	150	553	18

Note: Figures in parentheses: hereditary peerages (excluding promotions within the ranks of the peerage). Others: life peers.
Source: Figures for period to 1987 taken from Shell (1988), p.31.

Prime Ministers – particularly by Harold Wilson between 1964 and 1976 – to boost Labour's representation in the Lords. In 1958 the Labour Party had a mere handful of peers; half of the peers created between 1958 and 1979 (194 out of 391) were Labour members, an infusion which broke the Conservatives' absolute grip on the House for the first time in more than a century.

Hereditary and life peers between them make up more than 95% of the Lords. The remainder is composed of:

Archbishops and bishops. Twenty-six bishops of the Church of England have seats in the House of Lords until they retire: the two archbishops (Canterbury and York), the bishops of London, Durham and Winchester, and the next twenty-one most senior of the remaining bishops. For historic reasons, the Church of England is the only Christian denomination with direct parliamentary representation; nor is any other religion given similar privileges (though the present Chief Rabbi, Lord Jakobovits, was created a life peer in 1988 and thus has a seat in his own right).

Law Lords. Under the *Appellate Jurisdiction Act* of 1876 a small number of senior judges (now up to a total of eleven) are given life peerages with seats in the Lords. Generally known as the 'law lords', they are responsible, with the few other peers possessing appropriate qualifications (like the Lord Chancellor of the day and his predecessors), for conducting the judicial work of the House of Lords in its role as the United Kingdom's highest Court of Appeal. By convention 'lay' peers play no part in the judicial business, but the law lords themselves can and do participate in the ordinary proceedings of the Lords. They also remain members after retirement.

Working peers

With some 1,200 members, the House of Lords is almost twice the size of the Commons and more than twice as large as both Houses of the United States Congress put together. This absurdity is, however, more apparent than real. For barely two-thirds of the eligible membership have ever attended the Lords; and only some 400 peers attend more than a third of its sittings each session. These regular attenders are generally called 'working peers', since between them they transact most of the business of the Upper House.

Most 'working peers' are former MPs, full-time party politicians or former public servants, some of whom actually owe their peerages to nomination in one of the periodic lists of 'working peers' agreed by the party leaders to strengthen the active contingent in the Lords. Between them they conduct the greater part of the business of the House, both on the floor and in committees. But working peers have no special status as such. Any peer can participate in Lords proceedings at will. Working peers are not even paid a salary – though allowances paid for each sitting attended (however briefly) provide a peer 'attending' about three-quarters of the sittings of the House with an income of about £10,000 a year (at 1989 rates).

The predominance of life peers among working peers is clear from Figure 9.1. Life peers make up only a third of the House as a whole; but they accounted for more than 40% of those attending at least one sitting during the 1987/8 session, and by some way outnumbered hereditary peers (56% to 44%) in the 'working House' (i.e. those peers attending and participating regularly). The differential levels of activity by hereditary and life peers render the impact of the former on Lords business much less than might be assumed from their numerical predominance.

Figure 9.1 Background of working peers (percentages for 1987/8 session): a. All peers (1,185); b. Peers attending more than one sitting (836); c. Peers attending more than one-third of sittings (400)

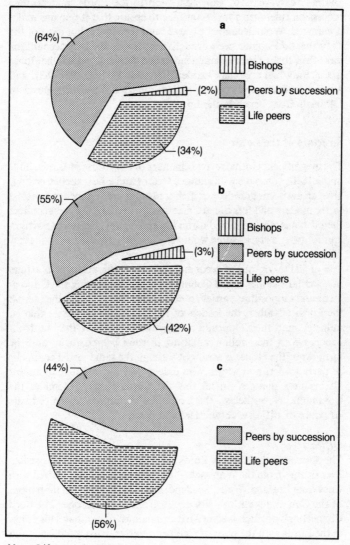

Note: Life peers include hereditary peers of first creation and law lords.

Women in the Lords

Women were first allowed into the Commons in 1918. They had to wait another forty years to gain admission to the Lords, and peerage succession rules (see above) continue to ensure that it remains male-dominated. Women comprise only 5% of the House, but most of the sixty-five-odd women peers are active members, and they account for more than 10% of the regular attenders and debaters. Indeed, the House has already had a woman Leader (Baroness Young, 1981–83), and women peers currently occupy nearly a quarter of the thirty posts on Labour's front bench in the Lords.

Structure of the Lords

The magnificent Gothic revival chamber of the House of Lords, built in the 1840s complete with statues, frescos and gold-panelled ceiling, gives an awesome grandeur to their lordships' proceedings unmatched by the modern and functional Commons. In keeping, the peers conduct their debates with a marked formality and dignity, devoid of partisan animosity – a stark, some would say healthy, contrast to the 'other place'.

For all the contrast of decor and style, the Lords arranges its affairs in a similar manner to the Commons. Peers supporting the Government and Opposition parties sit on benches facing each other across the Lords chamber; the leaders of the two major parties – that is, ministers and their Opposition 'shadows' – occupy the two front benches with their followers sitting in rows behind them; and the business of the House is arranged through the same 'usual channels' of party leaders and whips, who indeed take the initiative in almost all business matters. In all this the Lords closely resembles the Commons. Nevertheless, the Lords has certain peculiarities in its structure of officers, committees and parties.

Officers

The *Speaker* of the House of Lords is the *Lord Chancellor*, who presides over sittings from the Woolsack – an enormous cushion stuffed with wool from England, Wales, Scotland, Northern Ireland and the nations of the Commonwealth – situated in front of the throne. The Lord Chancellor's position is somewhat anomalous: be combines his duties in the Lords with the roles of Cabinet minister, party politician, and head of the judiciary. This might seem an impossible feat. But it works in practice because the Lords demands little of its Speaker; indeed he – or his deputy on the Woolsack – does virtually nothing besides formally 'put the question' to the House when a decision is required. The House itself regulates its own procedure and order; even the sequence of speakers in debate is decided either by an informal 'batting order' agreed by the whips beforehand or on a 'first rise, first heard' basis. And when formal guidance is needed, it comes not from the Speaker but from the Leader of the House.

The *Leader of the House of Lords* is, like the Leader of the Commons, is a cabinet minister and a party politician appointed by the Prime Minister. But he has a much broader role than his Commons counterpart. For in addition to organising the business of the House, the Leader of the Lords also acts as leader of the peers supporting the government, and as such he is the Cabinet's principal spokesman in the Upper House and acts as informal adviser to the Prime Minister on ministerial appointments and other matters involving peers. Moreover, the House as a whole looks to the Leader for guidance on procedural matters, and also regards him as its spokesman in relations with the government – particularly when the two Houses are in conflict. It is thus a delicate role, requiring tact and skill – qualities exemplified by the best known Leader of recent years, Viscount Whitelaw.

The *Lord Chairman of Committees*, a peer elected by the House as a whole, is a politically impartial officer who presides over committees of the whole House (with the assistance of a number of deputy chairmen). He also has responsibility for organising its other committees and plays an important role in the Lords' consideration of private bills. So far as administrative back-up is concerned, the House and its committees are serviced by a corps of professional clerks recruited through the Civil Service selection system and headed by an official with the grand title of *Clerk of the Parliaments*.

A number of other figures feature prominently in the work of the Upper House. The *Leader of the Opposition* is elected by peers supporting the party which constitutes the Opposition in the Commons (even if that party happens to be the largest in the Lords, as is invariably the case when the Conservatives are in Opposition). He is paid a salary and acts as 'shadow' Leader of the House. The Government and Opposition both appoint a *Chief Whip*, salaried officeholders who between them arrange the business of the Lords week by week in consultation with their leaders, the whips of the other parties and the 'convenor' of the crossbench peers (for whom see below). They regularly inform their supporters of pending business and encourage support for their respective parties in the division lobbies – though with less vigour and fewer sanctions with which to cajole the racalcitrant than their Commons counterparts. The current Government Chief Whip, Lord Denham, is a highly experienced operator, having served as Conservative Chief Whip continuously since 1978 (and Deputy Chief Whip for seven years before that).

Committees

The Lords has traditionally had little use for committees and its committee system is less elaborate, and far less important to its work, than that of the Commons. In particular, the Lords has no standing committees for the consideration of legislation. Instead, almost all bills are given detailed consideration by a *Committee of the Whole House*, which is simply the entire House meeting as a committee.

However, *select committees* have come to play an increasing role in the Lords. They have long been used to consider private legislation, and from time to time even for the consideration of major policy issues. For more than a decade now two permanent select committees have been in operation: the European Communities and Science and Technology Committees. The work and impact of these committees will be assessed in Chapters 10 and 11.

Partieb and crossbenchers

Peers face no elections and have no constituents. Party allegiance is a voluntary matter for them, except for working peers at the time of their appointment – and even they are free agents once appointed. Moreover, a significant number of peers, including some working peers, choose to remain independent of party political ties, and are known as *cross benchers* – because of the seats they occupy in the House opposite the Woolsack and between the two seats of facing benches.

For all that, political parties are integral to the work of the House of Lords. As can be seen from Table 9.3, more than two-thirds of all peers owning to firm political views support one of the major parties – and, as we shall see, even that figure overstates the influence of the 'independents' in the Lords. To take the groupings in the Lords one by one:

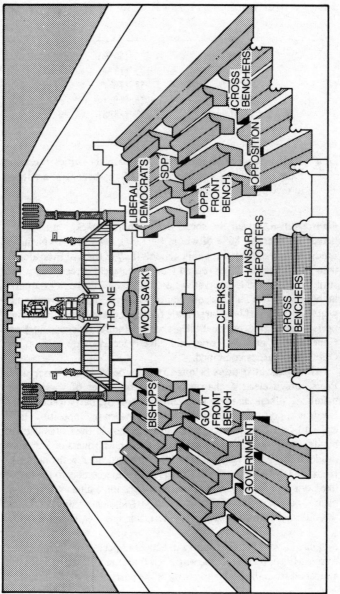

Fig. 9.2 The chamber of the House of Lords

Table 9.3   Party membership in the House of Lords (as at November
1988)

Conservative	425	(50%)
Labour	113	(13%)
Democrat	57	(7%)
SDP	23	(3%)
Crossbench	237	(28%)
Total	855	

Note: These figures are based on lists supplied by the parties, excluding
those on leave of absence. The 237 'crossbenchers' are those
in receipt of the 'crossbench whip'.

Conservatives. Given the social and economic background of the
hereditary peers – 86% of whom (in 1981), according to Nicholas
Baldwin, were educated at public schools (*half* of them at Eton alone),
with 78% engaged in (or retired from) a business career – it is not
surprising that the Conservatives are far and away the largest party
in the House. The Tory preponderance is less marked than even twenty
years ago, as a result of large-scale Labour creations; but half of all
peers expressing a political allegiance (including independents) are
Conservatives and the Tories still have twice as many peers as the
Opposition parties combined.

All Conservative peers belong to the Association of Conservative
Peers, which elects a chairman and a committee of some eleven
members. When the party is in Government, the party leader in the
Lords is appointed by the Prime Minister; when in Opposition, he is
elected by all Tory peers. Conservative leaders in the Lords used to
be lifelong 'House of Lords men' like the 5th Marquess of Salisbury
(leader from 1942 to 1957) and Lord Carrington (leader, with one break,
from 1963 to 1979). But in the past ten years newcomers to the Lords
like Lord Soames, Baroness Young and Viscount Whitelaw have taken
over – partly, perhaps, a reflection of Mrs Thatcher's dilution of the
'blood blue' with the eighty Tory peers she has created since 1979.

Labour. Labour has the support of some 113 peers, for the most part
former MPs or party activists, with a few trade unionists and academics,
almost all from the pragmatic wing of the party. As we shall see, they

make an impact disproportionate to their numerical strength, but they are mostly elderly and the party needs regular creations just to maintain its strength. When in Opposition, Labour peers elect their own Leader and Chief Whip, who sit in the 'Shadow Cabinet' along with one other elected peers' representative. But both are appointed by the Prime Minister when the party is in office.

Centre parties. The Social and Liberal Democrats and the SDP are proportionately stronger in the Lords than the Commons; indeed, as the Liberal/SDP Alliance between 1981 and 1987 they constituted a group almost as large as the Labour party in the House. A few hereditary peers support the centre parties (the SDP even has a duke − a quixotic gesture on his grace of Devonshire's part, no doubt) but the centre parties mostly rely on life peers and have benefited from a mere handful of creations since 1979.

Crossbenchers. Of the 300-odd peers who have taken their seats and are not on leave of absence, about 240 take the 'crossbench whip': that is, they receive the notice of business sent out by the 'convenor' of the crossbench peers, and are eligible to attend the periodic meetings of crossbench peers. The current convenor is Baroness Hylton-Foster. Her predecessor described his putative followers thus:

Some are genuinely non-party; some are retired public servants who have served governments of both parties. Some have definite party sympathies, but because they hold some public office prefer for the time being to lay aside their active party allegiance. Some are not in full sympathy with their parties. Some just do not like to be at the receiving end of a [party] whip. In our opinions we range widely from right to left.

The accuracy of portraying crossbenchers as a politically independent group will be questioned in Chapter 11. But they remain remarkable parliamentary phenomena by any standards and help give the Lords the air of a Council of State.

10

The House of Lords at work

Most of the world's parliaments have a second chamber. But no two second chambers are alike: each is the product of its country's traditions, circumstances and institutional evolution. Nowhere, however, is the result more peculiar than in Britain, where the House of Lords is largely hereditary, with not a single member elected by anyone; yet has evolved into a dynamic branch of Parliament with a standing enhanced in recent years. This chapter surveys the Lords' powers and functions, and goes beyond them to examine the House of Lords at work.

Powers of the Lords

The legal powers of the Lords are laid down in the *Parliament Acts* of 1911 and 1949, by which:

* The Lords has no power to amend or delay a Money Bill – that is, a measure certified by the Speaker of the House of Commons as dealing only with matters directly relating to the national finances.

* The Lords can delay any other type of public bill for up to one year. A measure so delayed then automatically becomes law, provided that it has been passed by the House of Commons in two successive sessions.

* The Lords retains an absolute veto over private bills, Statutory Instruments and bills to extend the life of Parliament beyond its statutory five-year span.

Until 1911 the two Houses had co-ordinate legal powers. It had, in fact, long been accepted that, ultimately, the will of the Commons was superior. But in the thirty years before the First World War the Lords, a bastion of the Church and the Tory aristocracy, was often in bitter conflict with reforming Liberal governments. Matters came to a head when the Liberal government elected with a landslide Commons majority in 1906 met with persistent obstruction from the Upper House; the consequent impasse turned into a major constitutional crisis when in 1909 the peers rejected David Lloyd George's celebrated 'People's Budget'. Asquith's Cabinet immediately introduced a bill to reduce the powers of the Lords. After two elections in 1910, both won by the Liberals, and a threat to swamp the Lords with Liberals if the peers continued to resist, the bill finally passed in August 1911. The 1949 Parliament Act, which reduced the Lords' powers to their present level, was introduced by Attlee's post-war Labour government because of fears that the peers might try to delay its nationalisation legislation.

The legal powers of the Lords are thus essentially a product of the political battles of more than eighty years ago. As such, they are a poor guide to the actual power wielded by the Upper House today. Indeed, the Lords virtually never exercises its formal rights of veto. Since the war the Parliament Act has been formally invoked only once: to pass the 1949 Parliament Bill. The *threat* of their use can be effective in certain circumstances, but they are extremely rare. The influence of the contemporary House of Lords derives not from its hypothetical veto but from its actual performance of its functions as a Second Chamber. It is thus with the peers at work that the rest of this chapter is concerned.

Functions of the Lords

The functions of the House of Lords are not defined by law; they are even not universally agreed in the Upper House itself – let alone outside, where the Labour party's official policy until its 1989 conference was to abolish the Lords and convert Parliament into a single chamber legislature. (Labour now proposes to retain the second chamber, but to replace the existing House with a completely different assembly – see p. 176.)

Even so, there is general agreement that the modern Lords has five principal functions:

1. *Deliberation*. The Lords is an arena for debate on matters of government policy and public interest.

2. *Revision of legislation*. The Lords is a revising chamber. It is able to consider legislation in a more leisured and less partisan fashion than the Commons, ensuring that it is properly drafted and giving promoters (usually the government) an opportunity to respond to criticism and propose changes accordingly. The Lords can also ask the Commons to reconsider issues which were inadequately discussed by MPs in the first place − or matters which, in its view, would benefit from further debate. Finally, the Lords often gives first consideration to essentially legal and/or uncontroversial government bills, to much private legislation and, of course, to bills proposed by individual peers.

3. *Scrutiny of the Executive*. The Lords provides a second forum for scrutinising policy and administration, particularly in fields (notably the European Community) where the Commons is weak.

4. *Supreme court of appeal*. The House of Lords is the highest appeal court in the United Kingdom.

5. *Consideration of delegated legislation*. The Lords considers (some) Statutory Instruments and other forms of delegated legislation.

Of the five functions, the first three are the most significant. The Lords' work as the ultimate appeal court is in fact undertaken exclusively by the Lord Chancellor and the law lords. With regard to delegated legislation, a joint committee of MPs and peers (seven of each) performs valuable scrutiny work, but it is very much a secondary activity. The sections below concentrate on deliberation, revision and scrutiny.

Deliberation

Debates on the floor of the House are the principal means by which the Lords deliberates on matters of public interest. About a fifth of the time of the House is taken up by deliberation (see Table 10.1) − a marked reduction on the proportion of time devoted to debates a decade ago, but still representing some thirty sitting days in an average session.

The Lords holds several different types of debate, to provide flexibility in deliberation:

* *'Full dress' debates*. About ten such debates take place a year, each lasting for a whole sitting − except for the debate on the

Table 10.1   Division of the time of the Lords

	1987/88	1983/84	1979/80
Question time	6	6	6
Questions leading to debate	5	7	8
General debates	14	18	19
Debates on EC reports	2	4	3
Legislation (Bills)	61	53	50
Statutory Instruments	5	4	5

Note: Percentages, rounded to nearest whole number, for the first session of the 1979, 1983 and 1987 Parliaments

Queen's Speech, which starts every session and usually extends to four days.

    * *Short debates*. About forty short debates are held, each lasting either three or five hours. Two are often held on the same day, and restrictions are sometimes imposed limiting the duration of speeches.

    * *'Take note' debates*. 'Take note' motions are devices for initiating debates on specific reports or government policy statements. They are frequently used as pegs on which to 'hang' debates on reports of select committees, especially those of the European Communities committee (which account for more than half of the twenty or so 'take note' motions moved each year).

    * *Debates on 'unstarred questions'*. An 'unstarred question' is, in form, a question to a minister, but the peer asking it does so in a speech and a short debate ensues before the ministerial reply is given. About forty unstarred questions are taken each session, usually at the end of a sitting, rather like adjournment debates in the Commons.

    To give an idea of Lords deliberation in practice, Table 10.2 shows the Lords debates held in the first half of February 1989. Notice, incidentally, that the two major debates were initiated by Lords Cledwyn and Boyd-Carpenter, respectively Leader of the Opposition and Chairman of the Association of Conservative Peers – a telling comment on the importance of party in the Lords.

Table 10.2   Lords debates, 1–14 February 1989

Date	Type of debate	Subject	Initiating peer
1 Feb	5-hour Unstarred question	Pollution	Lord Cledwyn (Lab)
		Infirm Elderly	Baroness Cox (Con)
7 Feb	Take note	Visual Display Units	Lord Allen (Ind)
8 Feb	Full dress	Sunday Trading	Lord Boyd-Carpenter (Con)
	un.qn.	Bradford: cuts in local services	Lord Dean (Lab)
13 Feb	un.qn.	Avebury World Heritage Site	Lord Avebury (SLD)

Quality and impact of Lords debates

Quantity of debate is one thing; quality and impact quite another. How do Lords debates qualify on the latter scores?

Quality. The capacity of the Lords to stage impressive debates across the range of public policy issues is undoubted – and probably equalled by few other assemblies. The Lords' membership, comprising as it does a host of active and retired public figures, distinguished academics and leaders of most of the professions, equips it for insightful deliberation on virtually any matter – not even excepting UFOs, about which the Earl of Clancarty (President of Contact International, the worldwide UFO movement) once initiated a full dress debate. (Lord Clancarty claims to be in communication with 'higher intelligences' and able to speak to them in a 'special language'; the *Hansard* report of the debate had the longest print run of any in recent years.) To take an example of a more down-to-earth policy sphere, speakers in a debate on higher education in April 1989 included one former Education Secretary, four past or present university chancellors (or equivalent), six past or present vice-chancellors or heads of colleges, ten professors and four college lecturers – a galaxy of higher education experts and administrators.

The *impact* of Lords debates is, however, less easy to assess. In so far as they oblige ministers, issue by issue, to state their policy and defend it against criticism, they contribute to the performance of one important parliamentary function: the maintenance of open and accountable government. But their impact on the *formulation* of government policy is more problematic. In the first place, the influence of the Upper House varies greatly from issue to issue. The Lords has an appreciable leverage in some policy areas, notably legal, rural and educational affairs, where the expertise of peers bears on issues which are often technical and uncontroversial (in party political terms, at least). Indeed, even when matters in these fields *are* controversial, the Lords can still exert a distinct influence. The most significant recent case in point was the Lords' April 1989 debate on the government's consultative proposals for reform of the legal profession. In a sitting lasting thirteen hours, the plans came under fire from a succession of legal peers, including three former Lord Chancellors, seven law lords, eighteen senior barristers and three solicitors. The Lord Chancellor (Lord Mackay) had hardly a friend in the House – not even on his own side – and the remarkable performance undoubtedly played a part in the substantial revision of the proposals announced three months later.

Even so, the law reform debate was highly exceptional, not least because the responsible minister was a peer and thus personally answerable to the Lords – whereas almost all other Cabinet ministers are MPs immune from Lords debates. Indeed, at any one time several departments will have no peer minister at all, and Lords debates on their activities are answered by junior ministers from other departments or by government whips, both alike able to do little more than recite a brief written for them by civil servants. In the 1987/8 session all government business in the Lords was transacted by three Cabinet ministers, eleven junior ministers and six Whips. Lord Trefgarne, a junior defence minister, also had to answer for employment, foreign and Welsh affairs; while the front bench remit of Baroness Hooper, an energy minister, extended to education and foreign affairs. 'Our difficulty in the Lords', according to Lord Cledwyn, Leader of the Labour peers, 'is that the government front bench is inevitably junior and somewhat inexperienced ... [and] the Opposition ... is to some extent crippled if ministers are unable to respond constructively.'

Moreover, whatever perceptible or imperceptible influence the Lords might have on the formulation of policy, it is virtually impossible for the peers to *compel* ministers to revise policy once it has statutory force. On a few occasions in the past decade the Lords has gone to the extreme length of passing a resolution condemning a particular policy. They have invariably concerned second-order matters (e.g. cutbacks in the funding of the BBC's external services, and the high level of top public sector pay awards), but despite that, *not once* has the government responded by changing the policy at issue.

Lords debates may not, therefore, be entirely without influence; but they rarely make an impact which is more than minor and indirect.

Revision

The Lords devotes more than half its time to considering legislation, almost all of it government bills. Its procedure for legislative scrutiny was explained in Chapter 5. To recap, every bill passes through the stages of *first reading* (which is purely formal); a *second reading* when it is debated in principle; a *committee stage*, when its provisions are considered line by line; a *report stage* when further amendments can be moved; a *third reading*, which offers a last chance to move amendments; and finally the motion 'that the bill do now pass' (usually a formality, but for major bills an opportunity for a brief debate on the final text). Once passed, bills return to the Lords only if there are outstanding differences between the texts agreed by the two Houses.

There are three distinctive features to legislative revision in the Lords.

1. *Principles of government bills are rarely challenged (the 'Salisbury Doctrine')*. The Lords recognises that it is a revising chamber and that governments derive their legitimacy from a majority in the House of Commons, behind which lies a mandate won at a general election. Peers thus never even vote on the second or third readings of bills and in their amendments they rarely seek to challenge the principles of government bills – though they sometimes ask MPs to reconsider particular matters about which they are concerned or believe there to be public disquiet.

This Lords' self-denying ordinance is sometimes called the *Salisbury doctrine*, after the 5th Marquess of Salisbury, who as leader of the Tory peers during the first majority Labour government (1945–51) – which, of course, had practically no supporters in the Lords – announced that the Lords would not seek to thwart the main lines of Labour's legislation provided it derived from the party's manifesto for the previous election. As Salisbury put it, in an interview with Janet Morgan, '[we decided] that where something was in the Labour Party manifesto we would regard it as approved by the country and we'd have Second Reading and amend it in Committee Stage. If they produced something that wasn't in the manifesto, we reserved the right to do what we thought best.'

It is not, of course, easy to determine precisely what constitutes 'principles', and in practice amendments are frequently moved in the Lords which affect them. Sometimes they are even voted through against government opposition, the most notable recent case of such defiance being the Lords' amendments to the present government's 1984/5 proposals to abolish the Inner London Education Authority and to suspend the Greater London Council and other metropolitan authorities prior to their abolition, both of which were withdrawn in consequence (but see p. 161). However, the Lords almost invariably backs down if its amendments are rejected by the Commons. The only occasions on which it has refused to do so in recent decades occurred during the first two session of the 1974–79 Labour government, and they were, as we shall see, highly exceptional.

2. *Commons financial privilege.* The Commons claims the sole right to determine matters affecting taxation, expenditure and government finances; and since 1911 the Lords has never formally disputed this claim. But the Upper House nonetheless often passes amendments with financial implications, particularly in the last few years. Most of the time the Commons turns a blind eye, but from time to time it claims 'financial privilege', and when it does so the Lords always withdraws the offending provisions. In the 1988/9 session, for example, the government was defeated by the peers on an amendment to the Social Security Bill which would have ensured that child benefit was uprated annually in line with inflation. The Commons rejected the amendment on a government motion and returned it to the Upper House with the explanation 'That this amendment might involve charges on public funds, and the Commons do not offer any further reason trusting that this reason may be deemed sufficient.' The Lords immediately withdrew the amendment, though not without murmurings of discontent.

3. *Committees of the Whole House.* In the Lords, in contrast to the Commons, the committee stage of every public bill is taken on the

Table 10.3 Lords amendments to government bills

Session	1946/7	1967/8	1977/8	1981/2	1985/6
1 Party in govt	Lab	Lab	Lab	Con	Con
2 Bills starting in the Commons	17	23	11	8	15
3 Amendments to (2)	996	1009	525	842	2167
4 (3) rejected by the Commons	53	87	157	0	4
5 Bills starting in the Lords	6	9	8	5	9
6 Amendments to (5)	43	361	356	467	265

floor of the House. Formally speaking, the House resolves itself into a 'Committee of the Whole House' for the purpose; but apart from somewhat less formal rules of procedure, the Committee is identical to the House itself. The time spent considering bills on the floor is considerable: in 1989, for example, the committee stage of the Water (Privatisation) Bill occupied sixty-two hours over eight sittings − equivalent to two entire weeks of the session. But it has always been the peers' practice to consider bills in this way and, as we shall see, it is unlikely to change.

Any peer may propose amendments to a bill in a Committee of the Whole House, but in practice most come from two sources. First, the Opposition parties, whose spokesmen will table numerous amendments to any controversial bill. When Labour is in office most such amendments are carried if pressed to a vote (which in fact only happens to a small number); by contrast, Conservative governments are defeated only some twenty times a session − small beer, perhaps, but still a large number in comparison with the Commons. However, it is the second source − the government itself − from which most successful amendments emanate. The number of amendments moved by ministers has increased markedly in recent years, and allowance must be made for this in interpreting simple totals of amendments made by the Upper House (Table 10.3). In the 1985/6 session, for example, the Lords made 2,432 amendments to government bills, a substantial increase on previous sessions; but two-thirds concerned only five complex bills, and almost all of them were moved by ministers.

Scrutiny

The Lords scrutinises the policies and administration of the Executive by means of the same instruments as the Commons, namely *questions* and *select committees*. But their application is rather different in the Upper House.

Questions

The Upper House has no equivalent to Commons Question Time, when departmental ministers are subjected to periodic sessions of oral questions on all aspects of their activities. Nor is there any regular duel between the party leaders on a par with Prime Minister's Questions. Instead, the first half-hour or so of each Lords sitting is taken up with up to four oral questions (called 'starred questions'), and this question period customarily attracts the largest attendance and liveliest scenes of the day. Any peer may ask a question, with appropriate prior notice; and after the answer has been given, supplementary questions are allowed. In all, some 600 oral questions are taken each year, but most are asked by a small number of peers (between 1983 and 1985 a mere six peers were responsible for a quarter of the questions asked in each session).

There are two other types of question in the Lords:

* *'Unstarred questions'*. See p. 143 above.

* *Questions for written answer*. Peers, like MPs, can table questions for written answer, and they are subject to the same procedure as in the Commons. Until recently comparatively few written questions were asked in the Lords, but in recent years the number has increased markedly (to more than 1,000 a session − see Table 10.4).

Table 10.4 Questions in the House of Lords, 1980−85

Type of question	1980/1	1985/6
Oral ('starred') questions	537	631
Questions leading to debate ('unstarred')	31	44
Questions for written answer	857	1182

Select committees

The Lords is an essentially 'chamber-oriented' assembly delegating few of its functions to sub-groups. Indeed, of the 800 or so peers attending the House each session, barely 130 sit on a permanent select committee or sub-committee (some 11% of the House as a whole − see Table 10.5). Only in its scrutiny work does the Lords make any extensive use of committees. From time to time the House establishes an *ad hoc* select committee to examine a major policy area − the three of particular note in the past fifteen years being the committees on a Bill of Rights (1977), unemployment (1981), charities (1984) and overseas trade (1984). They operate rather like Royal Commissions, taking evidence from a broad range of expert and interested opinion and reporting at length. Most of the Lords' committee effort is, however, directed through its two permanent select committees:

Table 10.5   Peers serving on one or more sub-committees of the Select Committees on the European Communities and Science and Technology

Party	No.	%
Conservative	38	30
Labour	29	23
Liberal−SDP	22	18
Crossbenchers	37	29
Bishops	−	−
Total	126	11

Note: Percentage of whole House.

1. *The select committee on the European Communities (EC)*. The EC committee was established in 1974 to report on Community proposals which 'raise important questions of policy or principle' and on 'other questions to which the committee considers the special attention of the House should be drawn'. The committee has twenty-four members, including a full-time, paid chairman, but its role is essentially only to decide which of the 700-odd EC documents deposited each month require scrutiny. The investigative work itself is carried out by six sub-committees, responsible for the following policy areas:

A – Finance, Trade and Industry and External Relations
B – Energy, Transport and Technology
C – Social and Consumer Affairs
D – Agriculture and Food
E – Law and Institutions
F – Environment

From time to time *ad hoc* sub-committees are set up to consider more general issues, recent examples including sub-committees on European Union, the staffing of the Community, and fraud against the EC. Between them, the committee and sub-comittees involve more than eighty peers who put in more than 3,000 'peer hours' a session in meetings alone; they receive back-up from a team of five clerks, a legal adviser, two specialist assistants, seven secretaries and three clerical staff. When conducting enquiries, the sub-committees take written and oral evidence from a broad range of sources, and Lords select committees have the advantage over their Commons counterparts that their reports are usually debated by the House itself. In all about twenty reports are issued each session, typically running to some 1,000 pages – far exceeding the output of any Commons select committee besides the Public Accounts Committee. The committee's remit extends across the whole gamut of Community activity, recent reports covering not only institutional issues like the Single European Act but subjects as eclectic as 'Standards for Simple Pressure Vessels' and 'Television Without Frontiers'.

2. *The select committee on Science and Technology (S&T)*. The Science and Technology committee was set up in 1979 when the Commons disbanded its equivalent. The committee's remit is simply 'to consider science and technology' and its reports have covered issues as diverse as 'Scientific Aspects of Forestry' and 'UK Space Policy'. Its operations are, however, more limited in scale than the EC committee. Investigative work is carried out by two sub-committees with about twenty-five members between them, which issue two or three major reports a year.

Ministers and whips do not sit on Lords select committees. But in contrast to the Commons, Lords committees only weakly reflect the party balance of the House as a whole. Experience and enthusiasm generally carry more weight than political affiliation in the selection of members. Anyway, Lords select committees rarely vote and it is highly unusual for one to divide on party lines.

The value of the work carried out by the two select committees is undoubted. The EC committee, in particular, has a high Community-wide reputation and is especially vital given the increasing importance of EC business and its comparative neglect by the Commons. The committee's impact is perhaps best summed up by its chairman, Baroness Serota:

it is difficult to measure the effectiveness of our scrutiny system ... (but) it seems that we have one of the most thorough scrutiny systems of all the member states' legislatures. As to its effect, we simply have to try. If we believe in the democratic process − perhaps that is a strange thing for an unelected member of the Upper House to say − surely we have a responsibility to analyse (European) proposals ... and attempt to influence our Government ... We cannot simply throw in the sponge.

But the influence of Lords select committees on the government at home is questionable. Like their Commons counterparts, they are largely ineffectual when intruding on matters of domestic political controversy, however cogent their reports. When, for example, in 1982 the EC committee reported in favour of British membership of the exchange-rate mechanism of the European Monetary System (EMS), citing weighty evidence it had gathered from economists, bankers and officials, the government nonetheless summarily dismissed the recommendations. According to Donald Shell, Lords select committees which challenge fundamental government policies 'cannot be expected to have immediate impact', but 'in the longer term they may contribute to a remoulding of informed public opinion'. Perhaps. But it is worth noting that eight years later Britain has still not joined the EMS.

The rejuvenation of the Lords

No survey of the modern Lords can fail to notice its remarkable revival in the past fifteen years. Thirty years ago, their lordships barely even made a pretence of serious, consistent activity. Today, by contrast, they believe themselves to have a definite role to play and are more assured and assiduous in their conduct than any time this century. Why the dramatic rejuvenation?

Five factors are largely responsible:

1. *Life peers*. The impact of the Life Peerages Act on the composition and vitality of the Lords was noted in the last chapter. Without the life peers – and also, perhaps, the increasingly generous attendance allowances – there would not have been sufficient 'activists' to man the Lords in the first place.

2. *Collapse of reform*. Until the late 1960s thoroughgoing reform of the Lords was widely anticipated, and not without reason. Macmillan's Conservative government passed both the Life Peerages Act and the 1963 Peerage Act, and toyed with more far-reaching schemes; only a few years later, Wilson's Labour government actually introduced a bill to completely recast the Upper House which was overwhelmingly endorsed by the Lords and only failed through obstruction in the Commons (orchestrated by that unlikely duo, Michael Foot and Enoch Powell). The Parliament (No. 2) Bill saga convinced the peers' leaders that reform had ground to a halt and that they had to make the existing House – strengthened with life peers – work as effectively as possible. As Lord Carrington, leader of the Tory peers, told the Lords: 'After all, it is not your Lordships' fault that you are unreformed.'

3. *The 1974–79 Labour government*. If adaptation was made *possible* by the influx of life peers, it was rendered *necessary*, in the view of peers across the political spectrum, by the legislation of the 1974–79 Wilson/Callaghan Labour government. After the October 1974 election Labour, with a Commons majority of only four, introduced a number of bills to extend nationalisation and enlarge the status and legal immunities of trade unions. Conservative, Liberal and crossbench peers questioned Labour's mandate and regarded this as an acid test of the Lords' utility. Though no measure was rejected outright, the Lords made significant amendments to most of Labour's bills. Some were actually carried by the defection of a few Labour MPs in the Commons; on some the Lords backed down; but on others they refused to, and two bills fell at the end of the 1975 session in consequence. Lord Carrington, urging the peers in November 1975 not to withdraw their 'press freedom' amendments to the 'closed shop' provisions of the Trade Union Bill, argued that the Lords was simply exercising its powers 'for the purpose for which they were given to us – that is, as an opportunity for further consultation, for second thoughts ... and because we did not want the Second Chamber to be associated with what the government are doing'. In the event, the Lords scored a few tactical victories

and not much more, while the Labour Party Conference made abolition
of the Upper House official Labour policy. But it was Mrs Thatcher's
Conservatives who won the subsequent election in 1979 and the Lords
survived unscathed.

4. *The Thatcher government*. In a decade of power achieved by three
successive election victories, Mrs Thatcher's Conservative government
has shown itself to be anything but 'conservative' in action. It has
carried through the most sweeping changes to Britain's social, industrial, economic and political structure since the 1945 Labour government – indeed, much of the Thatcher government's legislation has
been consciously aimed at dismantling the 'social democratic' edifice
created in the post-war years. A relentless privatisation programme has
virtually eliminated the nationalised industries, trade-union immunities
have been systematically curbed, local government has seen its role and
powers progressively emasculated, the welfare state has been whittled
away (albeit not as far as many Conservatives would like), and more
besides.

The programme has required legislation at every stage, and bill by
bill it has faced vigorous criticism in the Lords from Opposition and
crossbench peers, joined on occasion by disaffected Tories and
proponents of normally Tory vested interests. Chapter 11 will analyse
the impact of the Lords on Mrs Thatcher's government in detail; suffice
it to note here that the Lords has, at most, had a marginal impact. Be
that as it may, the impotence of Opposition parties and the numerous
pressure groups fighting for those at the 'receiving end' of government
policies in the face of the government's landslide majorities in the
Commons has made them all the more determined to use the Lords
to embarrass ministers and to seek to mitigate the effect of proposed
changes; and there has been no shortage of peers willing to fight their
causes. Nothing better exemplifies the peers' standing than Labour's
attitude to the Upper House. The party's policy in the 1983 election
was outright abolition. In 1987 that was replaced with a discreet silence
(indeed the 1987 election was remarkable for the tacit consensus on
the status quo in the Lords). By 1989 the wheel had come full circle
and Labour's policy review proposed retention with reform. Memories
of the 1970s have been all but effaced.

5. *Televising of the Lords*. Televising of Lords proceedings began on
an experimental basis in 1985, and the experiment was made permanent

a year later. The Lords was lucky that the Commons refused to admit cameras until 1989, giving them four years of limelight to themselves. Some 300,000 regularly tune into Channel Four's fifteen-minute late night summary and a further 200,000 to the repeat the following afternoon – enough to fill the Lords' public galleries for decades. When the Upper House voted to admit the cameras for good in May 1986, Lord Boyd-Carpenter – chairman of the Association of Conservative Peers – remarked that prior to televising the Lords had been seen as 'rather dull, rather stuffy and rather prejudiced on public issues'; but TV had brought about a 'public understanding and appreciation'. Another speaker pointed to the moral: the peers had been 'a threatened species'; now, 'I do not believe that a public which sees us in action will contemplate our destruction.'

The House of Lords today: an evaluation

Forty years ago the House of Lords was a wasted and powerless assembly. It had long since ceased to play any remotely significant role in government; and the hereditary peerage, of which it was almost exclusively composed, was a spent political force. With Labour in power after 1945, the peers faced a choice between submission and abolition; yet when the Tories succeeded, they found virtually nothing to do. As one observer put it cruelly, the Lords was dying in its sleep.

Now all that has changed, as over the past twenty years a rejuvenated Upper House has become one of the most active legislative assemblies in the world. The Lords rides high in popular esteem, and its apologists claim it to be a more effective parliamentary institution than the Commons. 'Ten years ago', as the former Northern Ireland premier Lord O'Neill told the Lords in May 1986:

if you had hailed a taxi and said, 'House of Lords, please', as likely as not you would be taken to the House of Commons. Now that very seldom happens. What is more, I find that taxi drivers are very interested in what is going on in your Lordships' House. The status and position of your Lordships' House has improved out of all recognition, and television is merely the latest example of your Lordships' enhanced situation.

And it is not only taxi drivers who have discovered the House of Lords. Opposition parties and pressure groups, in company with sundry nocturnal viewers of *Their Lordships' House,* have come to take the Upper House at least semi-seriously.

But what difference has the Lords' 'enhanced situation' made in practice? Is Britain witnessing a resurgence of bicameralism? Or have recent developments been overplayed? This chapter addresses these issues in an evaluation of the modern House of Lords.

The new orthodoxy

A new orthodoxy about the Upper House now reigns amongst commentators and academics. In summary it holds that over the past three decades, spurred by life peerages and other changes, the Lords has undergone an institutional transformation. Nicholas Baldwin, in a typical assessment, argues that today's peers manifest a 'new professionalism' and 'new independence', and the second is particularly emphasised as marking a 'growing assertiveness [by the Lords], not merely to amend legislation emanating from a Conservative government, but to change it considerably'.

The new orthodoxy is not, however, simply the creation of journalists and academics; it has been sedulously cultivated by the Lords itself. Club loyalty runs strong among the peers – not untypically for a threatened species! – and is strengthened by other factors. Labour peers, after years of derision from the rest of the Labour movement, flaunt their value as a bulwark against Thatcherism, while their centre-party colleagues occupy prominent positions in their parties' counsels (due to the shortage of centre party MPs), a prominence enhanced by the election of Lord (Roy) Jenkins as first leader of the Liberal Democrat peers in 1987. And Tory peers revel in a newfound reputation for rebellion. 'Weekly we rip great holes in legislation which the lower Chamber has carried by vast majorities and the guillotine', enthuses Lord Bruce-Gardyne. 'Assuredly no Tory government in modern times has been so consistently savaged by the watchdog once described as "Mr. Balfour's Poodle".'

Rhetoric apart, can today's Lords fairly claim to be either an 'independent' or a 'professional' Second Chamber?

An independent House?

The debate about the independence of the Lords comes down to one issue: does the Conservative party remain in effective control of the Lords?

The myth of independence

The party composition of the Lords is inevitably fluid and no figures for party support can be held to be applicable to all conditions. It was noted above that half of all peers taking a whip, including the crossbench 'whip', are Conservatives. But Tory strength in the 'working

Lords' is less marked than this raw figure suggests. Opposition and crossbench peers make up more than half (53%) of the regular attenders (i.e. peers attending more than one-third of all sittings: see Table 11.1); while among the most active members – those who speak regularly in the House – Conservative support falls to about 43% against a combined Opposition tally of 36%, with 17% for the crossbenchers. The assiduity of Labour and centre-party peers is striking. Three-quarters of Labour's peers and over half the Liberal Democrat/SDP group attend the Lords regularly; and they speak so frequently and are so active in all aspects of the work of the House that they have managed to create an impression of virtual equality with the Conservatives.

Table 11.1   Attendance at sittings of the House of Lords by party, 1987/8 session

| | >0%* | | >10%* | | >33%* | |
	No.	%	No.	%	No.	%
Con	437	49	290	48	189	47
Lab	119	13	105	18	92	23
SLD/SDP	79	9	64	11	50	13
Crossbenchers	221	25	131	22	69	17
Bishops	29	3	9	2	1	1
Total	885		599		401	

Note:* I.e. 'peers attending at least one sitting during the session'; 'peers attending at least 10% of sittings'; 'peers attending at least 33% of sittings'.

Such an impression is, however, seriously misleading. For even in the 'working House' the Conservatives easily exceed the combined forces of the Opposition in every branch of activity except speech-making. The Tories may no longer have absolute control of the Lords, but they are the largest party, commanding the support of 47% of regular attenders. And Conservative strength has become more, not less, marked in recent years: since 1979 Mrs Thatcher has created more than eighty Conservative peers, compared with fewer than fifty for the Opposition parties – breaking with the practice of previous Prime

Ministers, Tory and Labour, of creating more Labour than Tory life peers to redress the massive Conservative preponderance within the hereditary peerage.

Moreover, the statistics of lordly 'activity' usually cited are a poor guide to the political personality of the House. For whilst in the *working* Lords – that is, in debate and questions on the floor of the House – the Tories are indeed vulnerable, at the end of the debates it is the votes that count: and in the *voting* Lords – in divisions on amendments to government proposals, generally moved by the Opposition – the position is very different.

The 'voting Lords'

Only when the Lords votes does the Conservatives' inbuilt advantage reveal itself: a reserve army of mainly hereditary peers – the so-called 'backwoodsmen' – who attend irregularly but come up to London in large numbers when required by the Tory whips. This can be seen from Table 11.1: some 248 Tory peers attended one or more but fewer than one-third of Lords sittings in the 1987/8 session, compared with only twenty-seven Labour and twenty-nine centre-party peers respectively; and mostly they attended in response to requests from the Tory whips to help stave off possible defeat in the division lobbies.

In this context it should be emphasised that party cohesion in Lords voting behaviour is remarkably strong. Much is made by commentators (and whips themselves) as to the absence of sanctions available to discipline rebellious peers. However light the whip-hand, however, it is exceptional for more than a handful of Tory peers to defy the party whip even on the most controversial legislation. In the 1985/6 session, for example, in only three of the twenty-two votes lost by the government were the votes of Conservative defectors instrumental in the government's defeat; and in only four of the twenty-two did fewer than 90% of Conservative peers voting fail to support the government. Indeed, dissension expressed in adverse votes is hardly more pronounced in the government's ranks in the Lords than it is in the Commons; and since the Tories are far and away the largest party in the Upper House, this gives them substantial immunity from defeat.

Secondly, it is essential to realise that, despite their name and political self-image, the crossbench peers are collectively neither a pivotal nor an independent force in the Lords. In fact, they vote about two-to-one with the Conservatives; in only a handful of votes each session do they make the difference between the government winning and losing.

The reality of the voting Lords at work recently can be seen from Table 11.2, which examines Lords voting behaviour for the first two-thirds of the 1988/9 session. In that time fourteen major government bills were considered by the Lords: of the 129 votes on amendments proposed to them, the government won 119 (92%). Moreover, the average pro-government vote across the 129 divisions was 60%, and on *not one* bill did its average vote on amendments decline below 50%.

Finally, it should be emphasised that most government defeats in the Lords are either hollow or relatively insignificant victories for the peers. Far from 'thinking again' and making concessions

Table 11.2   Support for government legislation in the House of Lords, 1988/9 session

Bill	No of votes	No of govt defeats	Average govt vote (%)*
Prevention of Terrorism	3	0	68
Dock Work	6	0	68
Security Service	3	0	64
Official Secrets	6	0	62
Water (Privatisation)	46	2	61
Companies	8	1	61
Employment (Northern Ireland)	2	0	57
Elected Authorities (NI)	4	0	57
Football Spectators	12	1	57
Social Security	12	2	56
Children	7	0	56
Electricity (Privatisation)	15	3	56
Local Government	4	1	55
Control of Pollution	1	0	52
All legislation	129	10	60

Note: * The 'average government vote' is simply the pro-government vote in all the divisions on each bill divided by the number of divisions, as a percentage.

on issues at stake, the government reacts to more than half the defeats
– and to an increasing extent – by simply using its Commons majority
to reverse the Lords vote, and then calling on its 'reserve army' and
arguments as to the constitutional position of the Upper House to
ensure compliance in the Lords.* On not a single occasion since 1979
has the Lords insisted on one of its amendments once overturned by
the Commons; and even the one 'strategic' defeat inflicted by the peers
and accepted by the government – over its 1984/5 plans to abolish
the Inner London Education Authority and wind up the Greater
London Council and other metropolitan authorities before their
successor bodies had been established – turned out to be a Pyrrhic
victory. Within two years the GLC and metropolitan authorities had
been abolished; and ILEA's life was prolonged by only a few years
until it too was abolished by an act passed in 1988.

Thus whilst in the working Lords the Conservatives are the largest
party but short of an assured majority, in the voting Lords they possess
a clear majority and only in a narrow range of circumstances (outlined
below) are they vulnerable to defeat.

Degrees of independence

The government thus loses only a small proportion of votes in the
Lords: twenty-two out of 239 votes on government legislation in the
1985/6 session and ten out of the first 129 of the 1987/8 session. The
few defeats which actually occur can be attributed to various causes.
Some are purely accidental: every session the government loses a few
votes in divisions taking place early in a sitting when the whips are either
caught unawares or have underestimated their support (Ascot and
Henley weeks are also a bad time for reining in the backwoodsmen).
Beyond that, the government is vulnerable to defeat on a narrow range
of policy issues – mainly matters involving the disabled, the country-
side, pensioners and constitutional etiquette. Such topics are dear to the
hearts of a cross-party and crossbench majority, spurred on by active

---

* A typical case in point was a Lords amendment to the 1989 Companies Bill
which would have made political contributions by companies subject to a vote
by shareholders at their annual meetings. A sense of 'fair play' led the peers
to carry the amendment against the government; but ministers reversed the
defeat in the Commons, and when the proposal came back to the Lords, the
Conservative whips mustered an exceptionally large contingent of Tory peers
to ensure that the amendment was not revived (the move was defeated by
223 to 110).

pressure groups, and can sometimes cause problems in the division lobbies; but they rarely involve matters of much political consequence.

Explaining support for these special interests in the Upper House is not difficult. The Lords is packed with lawyers and the heads of charities, quangos and consumer organisations. Among its number are several disabled peers. And if there is one thing most peers have in common, it is old age. The mean age of the Lords in 1981 was sixty-two, with 73% of the life peers – the more active members – aged over sixty-five.

The fact that the Conservatives virtually control the Lords should cause little surprise, given its composition. The bishops and law lords play little part in either the 'working' or the 'voting' House. In its working form the Lords is an assembly of professionals, landowner–farmers and former MPs. It includes a large number of the very wealthy: thirty-eight of *Money Magazine's* 1988 list of Britain's 200 wealthiest people were peers, and members of the Lords are estimated still to own five and a half million acres between them. With such large landowning, City and professional contingents, the Lords is naturally a staunch defender of the free market and employers' and the professions' vested interests. When any of them – supported by the prevailing mood of the House and usually (though the third by no means invariably) by the Conservative party – conflicts with the particular lobbies referred to above, it is usually the interests, not the lobbies, which win the day.

A professional House?

A 'new professionalism' is the second feature of the 'new Lords'. The substance of the professionalism in question is never clearly defined, but most commentators appear to equate *professionalism* with *increased activity*. Thus Nicholas Baldwin writes of the post-1970 Lords: 'members have approached their work in a manner and with a determination previously unknown'; and he offers as evidence a table showing increased daily attendance, an increased number of sitting hours and days, and the fact that a larger number of sittings are lasting beyond 10 p.m. than was previously the case.

To take the latter points first, it is indisputably true that the Lords is now markedly more active than it was even twenty years ago, let alone in the 1950s and before. The peers sit for longer, debate for longer, fill more committees, ask more questions, move more amendments to legislation and vote in more divisions than ever before in the history of their House. Yet the fact that 300 or so peers are slaves to parliamentary duty does not in itself make the Lords *professional*. For activity and enthusiasm are not the same as efficiency and effectiveness. An assessment of the Lords' professionalism must turn on an analysis of the adequacy with which it performs its functions of deliberation, revision and scrutiny. And as will be shown below, the Upper House leaves much to be desired on that score.

Deliberation

The ability of the Lords to stage impressive debates on most areas of public policy, and to produce an array of national leaders and specialists for the purpose, was noted above. It makes the Upper House a remarkable deliberative assembly and, in this respect, gives it a fair claim to professionalism. Indeed, the influx of life peers has added to the debating breadth of the House, and new rules allowing for short debates and ensuring that shorter speeches are made in them have enabled the House to deploy its deliberative qualities more effectively. The televising of the House has, moreover, captured a wider audience for Lords debates than ever before.

However, this should be set against two features also noted in the last chapter. First, the impact of most Lords debates on government policy is minimal, and there is no evidence that it has increased in recent years. Secondly, the peers are spending progressively less time on deliberation as they have come to spend ever more time in considering government legislation. Over the past twelve years the proportion of the time of the House spent on general debates has halved – from 30% to 14% of sitting hours. If the principal strength of the Lords lies in its deliberative calibre, it is in danger of wasting.

Legislative revision

The Lords' effectiveness as a revising chamber is often assessed in terms of the length of time it spends considering government legislation and the number of amendments it makes to bills. Once again, though, failure to look behind the numbers gives a distorted impression.

Scrutiny of legislation now occupies more than half of the time of the Lords each session (in 1987/8 the proportion rose to a virtually unprecedented 60%). In itself this is a result of the commendable determination of 'working' peers, particularly Opposition members, to ensure that government bills receive adequate scrutiny – and in so far as it has forced ministers to spend longer explaining and defending their proposals than previously, it is a healthy development. But the very attempt to scrutinise legislation thoroughly has brought the peers up against a chronic weakness of their House: its antiquated procedures, in particular its lack of any legislative committees.

It was noted above that even the most lengthy and complex government bill has to be scrutinised line by line and clause by clause on the floor of the Lords, where any member can speak or move amendments. Procedure in Committees of the Whole House is stiltingly formal, order is lax, and debates on different stages of a bill (particularly the report stage) largely duplicate earlier debates. In practice, since the House does not even meet until mid-afternoon, this means that government bills are increasingly being 'scrutinised' far into, even through, the night, by a dwindling number of peers, most of them ministers or Opposition spokesmen simply reciting prepared briefs.

The increasing tendency of the Lords to vote on amendments, even when there is little or no chance of them succeeding, exacerbates the problem. For every vote in the Lords, however trivial the issue at stake, involves peers in tramping through the division lobbies (as in the Commons), as they have done for the past two centuries. Each vote takes about ten minutes to conduct; so a considerable proportion of the time the peers spend 'scrutinising' legislation is in fact devoted to walking back and forth along corridors. The 250 divisions in the 1985/6 session took some forty hours to conduct in all (the duration of about six entire sittings), with the fifty divisions on the Gas (Privatisation) Bill alone occupying about eight hours. 'There are', as Lord Beloff told the Lords in October 1986:

few legislative bodies in the world that command the range of expert knowledge that this House does, and even fewer which make so little use of it through their own procedures, notably what has now become the totally impracticable notion that the details of long and important bills can satisfactorily be considered in a committee of the whole House.

Yet any legislative committee system in the Lords would very likely fail for the same reason that they have failed in the past: namely, that to be effective committees must be clearly representative of their parent body, yet individual peers represent no one but themselves, and with a significant proportion even of active peers not taking a party whip it is impossible to constitute representative committees able to command the authority of the House.

Finally, another feature noted above is relevant in this context: the ministerial practice, which has now become almost habitual, of using the Lords as a long-stop for redrafting inadequately prepared legislation. Bernard Crick once suggested that 'the true function of the Upper House is to save time for the Commons'. Increasingly, though, the Lords is saving time not for the Commons but for the government.

Scrutiny

The Lords' effectiveness as a scrutinising chamber is problematic to assess. Certainly, more written and oral questions are being asked by peers than ever before; and recent years have seen the development of a Commons-style question time for the first thirty to forty-five minutes of each sitting. The impact of such mechanisms is, however, highly debatable. Question time in the Lords is largely a party-political point-scoring exercise engaged in by a small band of former MPs keen to generate some of the cut and thrust of the 'other place'. Moreover, the absence of 'responsible' ministers in the Lords means that oral questions are frequently answered by Whips or ministers not from the department in question, which makes them of limited use in ensuring accountability. The experience of the past decade in both Houses points unequivocally to the fact that effective, ongoing scrutiny of the activities of the executive requires committees specifically for the purpose.

Yet the Lords has no such committees. Its European Communities and Science and Technology committees have earned praise for the expertise and depth of their investigations, and rightly so. Between them, however, they provide no consistent scrutiny of the *British* government. The Lords has no departmental select committees to match those of the Commons, not even one to scrutinise the Lord Chancellor's department, which is unique in always being primarily accountable to the Upper House. Furthermore, scrutiny of subordinate legislation – Statutory Instruments and the like – is random and cursory in the Lords (as in the Commons). There seems to be a feeling among peers that duplicating Commons committees is undesirable; even the Science and Technology Committee was established only after the Commons had disbanded its equivalent. Be that as it may, in scrutiny above all else a prime justification for a second chamber is that it *does* shadow the work of the first, and such minimalist use of the resources of the Lords significantly reduces its claim to be considered professional.

Report on the working of the House

We come back, therefore, to the importance of distinguishing between activity and effectiveness. In equating professionalism with degrees of certain kinds of activity, commentators have not only failed properly to assess the Lords' performance of its functions as a Second Chamber; they have also gone some way to arguing that the House of Lords is more professional *because it is increasingly like the House of Commons*. They have been right to identify this trait in the Upper House. An important consequence of the influx of life peers, particularly working peers – a large proportion of whom are former MPs and professional politicians – is that the Lords has increasingly adopted the style and practices of the Commons. The Labour frontbench has played a particularly significant role in this: all but one of Labour's thirty frontbench spokesmen in 1988 were life peers, twenty-four of them created within the previous ten years and most of them former Labour MPs (several of whom left the Commons involuntarily). Many of them have unashamedly sought to create a 'Commons atmosphere' in the Lords; and their success should not be mistaken for the transformation of the Upper House into a professional second chamber.

A number of peers are concerned at the weaknesses of their House, so much so that in 1986 an all-party group, chaired by Lord Belstead (the current – 1990 – Leader of the Lords), was set up to investigate the 'working of the House'. The group reported in autumn 1987 (HL Paper no. 9, 1987). It noted the increased pressure on the House, and the fact that many peers believed that new burdens were overloading it to an alarming degree. Yet the limited experiment in the previous session with a standing committee to take the committee stage of a bill away from the floor of the House was deemed unsuccessful and only to be revived, if at all, with a minor measures. Perversely, the group then quoted Lord Carrington's warning to the Lords' Procedure Committee in 1976, that 'if we send unimportant bills up to this committee, it is not going to save time because they would not have taken up much time in the House'.

The same attitude was taken to select committees. The all-party group noted the criticism of excessive concentration on European affairs and inadequate scrutiny of domestic policy spheres. But rather than recommend any changes, the group simply concluded that pressure on the House from the 'numerous' existing committees precluded any expansion in the committee structure.

Complacency gave way to self-congratulation in the group's final summary:

We conclude that external pressure should not force the House to amend its fundamentally successful procedures, and concur with the response by one Lord to our questionnaire: 'In a nutshell I think that the Lords works remarkably smoothly and that it has done invaluable work in the last few years. Any changes in procedure should therefore be minor in character and interfere as little as possible.'

Conclusion

In the 1950s the House of Lords came close to fulfilling Bagehot's prophecy that its demise would result not from abolition but from atrophy. Neither is any longer in prospect. Life peers and post-1960s developments have given the peers a remarkable vitality and self-confidence, and an assurance that they are no longer at the back of the parliamentary stage threatened with redundancy. Yet the 'new' Lords retains the principal characteristics of its 1960s predecessor. It continues to exhibit fundamental weaknesses as a Second Chamber, and the voting (if not the working) Lords is still dominated by the Conservative party.

'It is because this House is not a rubber stamp', according to Lord Cledwyn, leader of the Labour peers, 'that it has gained the approbation of so many people.' The Lords may no longer be a rubber stamp, but neither has it provided anything but minor obstructions to the government's legislative programme. The few defeats of any consequence inflicted on ministers by the peers have been little more than tactical setbacks, the most serious of them turning out to be hollow. For the most part, Mrs Thatcher's economic and social priorities are enthusiastically endorsed by the Upper House. The peers are only concerned that proper procedures are followed, constitutional etiquette respected, and existing rights maintained where they are not incompatible with the government programme.

Walter Bagehot wrote of the House of Lords in *The English Constitution*:

With a perfect Lower House it is certain that an Upper House would be scarcely of any value. If we had an ideal House of Commons ... it is certain we should not need a higher chamber. But though besides an ideal House of Commons the Lords would be unnecessary, and therefore pernicious, beside the actual

House a revising and leisured legislature is extremely useful, if not quite necessary.

That remains the case today. At best, today's Lords is a Council of State: a forum and focus for expert opinion and a dedicated revising assembly. At worst, it now makes a passable House of Commons on a dull day.

12
Whither Parliament?

What is the state of Parliament at the start of the 1990s? Preceding chapters have analysed the workings of Parliament today; this last chapter assesses the prospects for reform, and offers some general thoughts on the state of parliamentary government in Britain. In the first place, however, it is essential to understand the context of political change in Britain, and the opening section is by way of introduction.

The myth of the flexible constitution

'British Government', J.P. Mackintosh once remarked, 'is overlaid with myths which are repeated again and again by the participants themselves.' Of them, none is more fantastic, yet repeated more often, than the claim that the British political system is peculiarly adaptable to changing circumstances. *Ad nauseam* it is proclaimed that that magical English quality, pragmatism, applied to Britain's unwritten and easily alterable constitution, has crafted a set of political institutions ever evolving to meet the needs of the times. To apply the metaphor which invariably adorns the myth, new wine is continually pouring into old bottles; and for all that the vintage defies the connoisseurs, it is supposed to provide ample satisfaction for the governmental demands of the British people.

Whatever the truth of the latter assertion, the central claim of flexibility is a myth long overdue for explosion. In reality, the institutions of British central government have proved chronically resistant to change throughout this century. Since 1945 Britain has lost an empire, ceased to play in the international first division and been compelled by its economic and strategic predicament to enter the European Community; yet its core political infrastructure remains substantially unchanged from that in place on the resignation of Lloyd George in 1922. Even today's party system, constrained by an electoral system long abandoned by the rest of Europe, bears a striking resemblance to that of the mid-1920s, with not one new party having sustained a breakthrough in the interim.

The myth of the adaptable constitution would merit no more than a passing footnote were its impact not so profound on those actually engaged in the business of politics. So far as Parliament is concerned, the myth has two particularly striking effects. First, it leads politicians and commentators to dismiss proposals for systematic reform *a priori* as somehow 'unEnglish' and out of sympathy with the evolutionary character of Britain's constitution. And since Britain's principal political 'actors' – most notably the politicians at the head of the major parties – have a vested interest in maintaining the existing system, the myth has a self-serving quality about it: indeed, in the absence of manifest popular discontent with 'the system', the assertion that minor incremental changes *are* sufficient to meet the exigencies of the day has become virtually a self-fulfilling prophecy. Secondly, and perhaps largely in consequence, comes an acute hostility to any idea that Britain could learn from the experience of other industrial democracies. Thus Philip Norton, in the conclusion to his *Parliament in the 1980s*, dismisses overseas experience in a single sentence ('foreign experience provides little useful guide to what could or should be done in Britain'); reform has, rather, to be seen 'within the context of the British political culture', with schemes deriving from any 'alien political culture' to be rejected as 'a potentially disastrous exercise'.

Two assumptions are implicit in this view – namely, that the institutional practices of one country are, appropriately adapted, incapable of application to another, and that the existing structure is indisputably that best suited to the promotion of prosperity, democratic participation and effective government in Britain. Both assumptions are highly dubious, but even leaving them aside, the conventional wisdom involves a perverse interpretation of the actual course of Britain's constitutional evolution. Pragmatic it has certainly been. In Gladstone's words to the Commons on introducing his great Reform Bill of 1884:

ideal perfection is not the true basis of English legislation. We look at the attainable; we look at the practicable; and we have too much of English sense to be drawn away by those sanguine delineations of what might possibly be attained in Utopia, from a path which promises to enable us to effect great good for the people of England.

Yet until recent decades British constitutional pragmatism was rarely synonymous with conservatism, still less with insularity. On the contrary, Gladstone himself justified the introduction of single-member parliamentary divisions – still the most radical post-1832 reform of the electoral system to date, franchise extension apart – by arguing that whilst the arrangement was 'as far as England is concerned almost a novelty', it was nonetheless the 'general system of Europe' and, moreover, 'the whole of the representative systems of the civilised world which have this single-member system do not show the least desire at present to get rid of it'. Gladstone's receptivity to such 'alien' influences was not simply a matter of intellectual persuasion. The 'general system of Europe' supplied the inspiration; but significant external pressures combined with nice calculations of party advantage – *realpolitik*, in a word – provided the motive force. Britain's recent constitutional immobilism is largely the product of the relative weakness of these forces since the First World War. To be sure, countervailing pressures applied sufficiently in the 1970s to take Britain into the European Community and almost to secure devolution for Scotland and Wales; but the latter collapsed, and even the former was a close-run thing.

It looks distinctly possible, however, that the conditions necessary for major structural change – significant external pressure, a clear reform agenda and calculations of partisan advantage – may be present in the 1990s to an extent unprecedented since 1945. First, the agenda: Labour's Policy Review, endorsed as official party policy by the 1989 Brighton Conference, commits one of the major parties to a programme of constitutional reform which, though cautious, is more extensive than any put forward by a government or Opposition for more than seventy years. The calculations of party advantage are not hard to find: a decade in opposition to the most radical Conservative government in a century has tempered Labour's traditional conservatism in matters constitutional as never before. In any case, Labour faces – or at least fears – stiff electoral competition in its Scottish heartland from Nationalists advocating Scottish independence; and the party has had to respond not only to that, but more generally to the surge of 'thinking liberal' opinion in favour of constitutional revision, graphically illuminated – not least in Labour's own ranks – by the Charter '88 campaign.

The Conservatives may not lose the next election, of course; but they are not electorally immortal, and each Tory victory fortifies Labour's conversion to constitutional reform – indeed, a fourth term for Mrs Thatcher might even induce it to embrace causes currently taboo, like a Bill of Rights and electoral reform.* Furthermore, external pressures for institutional change are making an impact on *both* parties. Regional disaffection may affect Labour particularly; but significant developments in the European Community are a present reality to which the Conservatives are having to respond in government. And as we shall see below, on both fronts external pressures are likely to increase, not diminish.

For all this, it would be rash to suggest that major changes are imminent. After generations of growth, constitutional conservatism is deeply embedded in the British political psyche and will not easily be shaken. Nonetheless, the potential for significant reform exists, and the following sections examine its possible ramifications in three key areas: the House of Lords, devolution and relations with the European Community. Before that, however, the two most likely fields of 'internal' reform – procedural 'tinkering' and developments in the Commons committee system – are examined.

Tinkering

Many of the proposals found under the heading 'parliamentary reform' in fact involve little more than tinkering with the parliamentary machine: not that they are necessarily unimportant in themselves, simply that they imply no major alterations to Parliament's structure and hierarchies. Among those most often put forward are:

* *Timetabling of bills*. The proceedings of standing committees on major bills have long been a cause of concern – unsurprisingly, given the almost farcical nature of the activities portrayed in Chapter 7. By way of remedy, the Procedure Committee recommended in 1985 that a new 'legislative business committee' should be invested with powers to set a timetable for each bill's consideration *before* its submission to a standing committee. The plan fell foul of the frontbenches and was rejected by the House itself in 1986; but with the guillotine in even

---

* Support for electoral reform has been gaining ground rapidly in Labour and trade union ranks, despite the hostility of the party leadership. At the 1989 conference a pro-PR motion was lost on a vote of 1,443,000 to 4,592,000; but more than forty constituency parties presented resolutions in favour, and the constituency parties as a whole divided almost equally for and against PR.

more frequent use since then, the scheme – or something like it – will doubtless reappear before long.

* *Electronic voting*. The ritual of voting by filing through division lobbies is one of the more bizarre parliamentary survivals from past centuries. It is also immensely time-consuming: the 496 Commons divisions of the 1987/8 session took some 107 hours to conduct, equivalent to twelve entire sittings. Since Congress abandoned its voting lobbies in the 1970s Parliament has been virtually alone among legislatures in maintaining them; sooner or later modernity will dawn and some form of electronic voting will be introduced in both Houses.

* *More rational hours*. According to Paul Silk, the *average* time at which the Commons adjourns (Friday apart) is between midnight and 1 a.m. Yet MPs' passion for nocturnal debating may be on the wane, with surveys showing a majority in favour of a fixed cut-off of business at 10 p.m. However, any such change will involve reassessing use of time on the floor of the House, since there would be little support for bringing forward the meeting time from its present 2.30 p.m. – morning sittings interfere with committees and with MPs' and ministers' other activities.

* *Better facilities*. MPs' remuneration and facilities have improved dramatically in the 1980s, but Parliament is still the poor relation of Western legislatures. An *Economist* survey in September 1989 estimated comparative costs of legislatures at $220 million a year for Britain, $292 million for France, $326 million for Japan, $453 million for the European Parliament, and $1,050 million for the US Congress (or more than $2 billion if agencies like the Congressional Budget Office and the Library of Congress were included). The US figure is hardly to be regarded as a target – indeed Congress itself is trying to reduce it – but there is still plenty of scope for improvement in the Commons. A separate office for each MP, an allowance sufficient to employ two full-time assistants, and free telephone, postage and travel facilities to European Community institutions (none of which, incredibly, are currently available to MPs) – these might be goals attainable in the next decade.

'Chinese Walls'

When the Commons' departmental select committees were established in 1979, their founder, Norman St John Stevas, lauded them as instruments for 'altering the whole balance of power between

Westminster and Whitehall'. Ten years on, their achievements have been far more modest, but in Chapter 7 it was suggested that the committees have formed something akin to 'Chinese Walls' in the Commons, effecting a partial separation of the scrutiny from the partisan and arena activities of the House.

To be sure, the Chinese Walls are still pretty flimsy constructs, vulnerable to complete collapse when MPs fail to appreciate their strength and the behavioural constraints which must be respected for them to be effective. Nonetheless, the extent to which backbenchers are resolved and able to strengthen the Chinese Walls is likely to be the critical dimension of internal reform in the Commons over the coming decade. Both their resolution and ability will turn in part on 'external' changes, like devolution and electoral reform; but even without them, the advent of a 'hung Parliament' (i.e. a Commons in which no party has an overall majority) or simply a change of government − it was the last such change which brought the departmental select committees into being in the first place − might provide a stimulus. Irrespective of either, however, more immediately pressing factors, notably the exigencies of responding to developments in the European Community, could well lead down the same road.

Whatever the motive force, strengthening the Commons select committee system is likely to take one or more of three forms:

* *Special standing committees*. Since 1980 it has been possible for the House to refer bills to a 'special standing committee' between their second reading and committee stages. Under this procedure, a standing committee operating rather like a select committee − i.e. taking oral and written evidence and deliberating upon it − meets for up to four sessions before the routine standing committee deliberations begin, enabling members to acquire an informed view of the issues involved before they begin the detailed business of scrutiny. As for their impact, Paul Silk cites the reaction of a minister in charge of one of the few bills to go before a special committee, who remarked afterwards that it was 'very remarkable how the operation of the special procedure stimulates the interest of members of the committee, and brings them together even though their respective opinions may remain sharply divided'. Provision for special standing committees was formally incorporated in Commons' Standing Orders in 1986; but since then no bill has been referred to one.

* *Strengthening of existing select committees*. Suggestions include a greater role for select committees in the scrutiny of European

legislation – perhaps through the creation of new committees (see below) – and better provision for scrutinising financial administration.

* *Legislative functions for select committees.* The most radical reform of all would be to give departmental select committees legislative as well as scrutiny functions; at the extreme, for all bills to be referred automatically to their departmental select committee or a sub-committee constituted for the purpose. Select committees might, in Gavin Drewry's words, 'actually be compromised if [they] were to become part of the processing – as opposed merely to the scrutiny – aspect of legislative business'. In existing conditions that is un-doubtedly correct, and anyway no such scheme is in prospect. But something like it could conceivably develop, perhaps following on from the wider use of special standing committees.

The House of Lords

The preamble to the 1911 Parliament Act includes a commitment 'to substitute for the House of Lords as it at present exists a Second Chamber constituted on a popular instead of hereditary basis'. Eighty years later, that substitution has still to take place. The post-1958 influx of life peers has somewhat diluted the aristocracy; but the powers of the Upper House remain those granted it by the Parliament Acts of 1911 and 1949, the possession of a peerage remains virtually the sole qualification for membership, and the peers' role has changed hardly at all since the war.

Textbooks often list 'arguments for and against the House of Lords', as though its survival were somehow the outcome of rational debate. In fact, the peers' continued existence is simply the consequence of lack of agreement as to who, if anyone, should take their places. Not that there has been any shortage of schemes for reform: on the contrary, hardly a year passes without the publication of a handful, and since 1945 governments of both parties have seriously considered re-structuring the Upper House. Harold Wilson's 1964–70 Labour government actually introduced legislation – the Parliament (No. 2) Bill, drawn up by Richard Crossman – for a nominated second chamber with functions and powers broadly similar to those of the present Lords, only to see it fail through cross-party opposition on the floor of the Commons. The Parliament Bill apart, however, Labour's attitude to the very existence of the Upper House has been at best ambivalent: the party's left wing has long favoured outright abolition, and succeeded in making that official party policy between 1977 and 1989. The Conservatives, by contrast, waver between support for the status quo, which gives them effective control of the Lords, and occasional flirtation with thoroughgoing reform as a means of strengthening the powers of the Upper House. The Tory peers have long supported the latter course; but their party leadership has taken it up only when Labour has actually been in power, and even then it has steered clear of making any formal manifesto commitments.

It is essential to realise that behind − indeed in no small part the cause of − this dissension on the *composition* of the Lords has lain broad agreement, excepting only the Labour left, on its *functions*. For it has generally been taken for granted that the job of the second chamber is simply to revise − that is, to save time for MPs and make up for the deficiencies in Commons procedures. To do that, the Upper House needs to be able to ask the Commons to reconsider legislative proposals from time to time, perhaps even in exceptional circumstances to delay them for a short period; but its role is essentially to complement, not to rival, the Lower House. Put thus, it is easy to see why the Lords' composition is so problematic. For popular election provides the only clearly defensible basis for a modern legislative assembly: yet an *elected* second chamber, whatever its formal role and powers, could well in practice come to claim a mandate of its own and seek to compete with, not complement, the Commons. On the other hand, any system of appointment is fraught with objections. Who is to appoint whom? Most of the working membership of the Lords is already appointed in any case. It may be that this patronage should not be in the sole gift of the Prime Minister, but there is no agreement as to who could dispense it better.

Similar considerations may prolong their lordships' collective life for another eighty years yet. There is, however, one indication to the contrary: the current debate about an enhanced *role* for the Upper House. For Labour has clearly decisively abandoned its support for abolition, and its Policy Review may come to be at least the catalyst of serious reform. For the Policy Review advocates a new second chamber with a duty to 'protect and preserve' a defined set of 'basic rights'. Though its powers would, ordinarily, be limited to requiring MPs to reconsider specific matters before a bill could become law, it would have a much greater say over legislation affecting the basic rights. Indeed, the Review suggests that the second chamber might be empowered to delay such measures, along with proposals to tamper with the new national and regional assemblies the party proposes to establish, for the whole life of a Parliament, 'thus providing an opportunity for the electorate to determine whether or not the government which proposes such measures should remain in office'.

Labour's plans remain sketchy. The 'basic rights' are not enumerated. It is intended – significantly – that the new second chamber should be elected, but the only hint as to how is a statement that members ought to be chosen in such a way as 'particularly [to] reflect the interests and aspirations of the regions and nations of Britain'. Nonetheless, for once debate on new functions is preceding schemes for a new composition; and if Labour is serious about a second chamber with the role it suggests, composition may prove the least of its problems.

Regional pressures

The past twenty-five years have seen a marked, if fitful, eruption of nationalist politics in Scotland and Wales. Nationalism has deep cultural roots, and similarly strong regional variations, in both countries, despite the stronger role of language in Wales. However, its political impact has been consistently greater in Scotland and it is there that demands for *devolution** are most pronounced. The intensity of nationalist sentiment should not be exaggerated: a 1987 MORI poll found that only 4% of Scots considered 'devolution' to be 'one of the two most important' of that year's election issues (unemployment and the health service came top). Even so, the great majority of Scots – and probably a majority of the Welsh – support devolution; indeed, the same poll found that 55% of SNP supporters favoured outright independence for Scotland, as – more significantly – did also 36% of Labour voters.

---

* 'Devolution' refers here to *legislative* and *executive* devolution, i.e. the delegating of some lawmaking and governmental authority from Parliament to national or regional assemblies. *Administrative* devolution has already been granted to Scotland, through the Scottish Office (set up in 1885), headed by a cabinet minister (the Secretary of State for Scotland). Wales also has its own department and cabinet minister, though much of its administration continues to be handled by the English departments. Northern Ireland is, as ever, a case apart: the NI Office, presided over by the Secretary of State for NI, took over the administrative structure of the former Stormont government at the institution of direct rule in 1972, and neither of the major British parties supports legislative devolution to NI whilst sectarian strife remains unabated.

Enthusiasm for nationalist parties and policies has been cyclical since the 1960s. But both received a marked boost in the late 1980s as Scotland and Wales turned sharply against the ruling Conservatives, yet were nonetheless treated to the same brand of Thatcherism as the rest of the United Kingdom: indeed, the 'poll tax' (or 'community charge'), the single most unpopular of the government's reforms, was actually introduced first in Scotland. The *démarche* has been truly dramatic. In 1987 the Conservatives won only eight seats in Wales (21%) and ten in Scotland (14%) – the latter their worst result north of the border since 1910. Labour was the principal beneficiary, taking twenty-four seats in Wales and fifty in Scotland. And since 1987 the Tories have fared still worse in the face of marked Nationalist revival. In the 1989 European elections the SNP took 26.9% of the Scottish vote and came clearly second in Scotland (Labour gained 40.8%), and in Wales Plaid Cymru secured 12.9% (with Labour on 49.7%) – figures reminiscent of October 1974. Moreover, the Nationalists may be doing more than simply riding the crest of an anti-Tory wave: in particular, the SNP's catchy slogan of 'Independence for Scotland in Europe' has achieved a credibility that the militant separatism of the 1960s and 1970s was never able to match.

A third of all Labour MPs sit for seats in Scotland and Wales, and the nationalist surge has been reflected in their ranks as much as in swings to the Nationalists. The impact is clearly evident in Labour's Policy Review. The party is now committed to a directly elected Scottish assembly with extensive legislative and tax-raising powers, in both respects significantly greater than those conceded in 1978. It also advocates 'directly elected legislative and administrative assemblies' for England and Wales, 'to take over many of the functions now carried out by national government'. Regional devolution in England would be an extraordinarily radical departure, but Labour's plans appear to be at least partially inspired by the decentralisation schemes pioneered in the 1980s in most other non-federal states in Western Europe. Indeed, the Policy Review actually cites the experience of Italy, France and Spain to support its contention that 'regional consciousness develops as its value is perceived and as it secures local interest'. In these three countries, decentralisation was to a greater or lesser extent driven by regional pressures; but in each case it owed much to the experience of European neighbours and to existing traditions and administrative structures at the sub-national level. Britain's cities and regions are not lacking in such traditions and structures, and as its politicians come to regard the European mainland as less 'alien' than they once thought, an increasing number appear increasingly prepared to contemplate dismantling the unitary state.

The European Community

The process of European integration is proceeding at a faster pace than at any time since the years immediately before and after the Treaty of Rome. The European Monetary System (EMS), the Single European Act, the resolve to complete the internal market by the end of 1992 and the Delors Report on economic and monetary union (EMU) – taken together, these and a host of other initiatives and subterranean developments are engineering a transformation of the Community inconceivable only a decade ago. And if anything, the pace is quickening. Hardly a month now passes without some ambitious new initiative from the European Commission. 'History is speeding up, so must we', M. Delors, the Commission's president, told the College of Europe in October 1989, emphasising that 'acceleration' was the only effective response to the revolutions in Eastern Europe, and that it could only come about through 'the reinforcement of certain federalist traits'.

Even discounting further 'acceleration', the implications of changes already agreed, or in train, are only belatedly appreciated in Britain. Nothing better exemplifies the 'Community ignorance' of MPs, and their powerlessness once informed, than parliamentary proceedings on the Delors report on economic and monetary union. The government agreed to the establishment of the Delors Committee in June 1988 without so much as a single debate in the House of Commons. In mid-April 1989 the committee reported in favour of a three-stage process ending in full economic and monetary union. Little over two months later, the report was laid before the biannual meeting of the EC's heads of government (held in Madrid) for decisions as to its implementation. In the interim, MPs held *not one* debate on the report or related issues. To be sure, the Commons Treasury and Civil Service Committee issued a hasty report a few days before Madrid (4th report, 1988/9), and attempted to ring the alarm bells:

The power of the House of Commons over the centuries has depended fundamentally on the control of money, both taxation and expenditure. This would be jeopardised by the form of monetary union proposed by the Delors Report which would involve central undemocratic direction from within Europe of domestic budgetary policies.

Tant pis. Despite the Prime Minister's well rehearsed objections, the Madrid summit resolved – Mrs Thatcher acquiescing – its 'determination progressively to achieve economic and monetary union' on the lines of Delors, and agreed that the first stage, necessitating British membership of the exchange-rate mechanism of the EMS, should begin in July 1990, with an intergovernmental conference of the Twelve planned thereafter 'to lay down the subsequent stages' to full monetary union, complete with arrangements to establish some form of central bank and 'binding rules' on fiscal policy. The British government's action alarmed the Commons Treasury Committee still further; it took the unusual step of publishing a report over the 1989 summer recess deploring the loose wording of the Madrid *communiqué* and the absence of prior parliamentary consultation. 'If the government attaches significance to arguments about the sovereignty of Parliament', the committee remarked acidly, 'it ought not to be selective in its attachment to them.'

The sovereignty of Parliament notwithstanding, the more immediately pressing concern for the Commons lies in its own relations with Brussels.* In the spring of 1989 the Commons Procedure Committee set up an urgent enquiry into the 'scrutiny of European legislation', its first since the Foster committee of 1973. In evidence, particular concern was voiced about:

* *Inadequate scrutiny of European legislation*. At present the Commons undertakes no more than a somewhat random and superficial *post hoc* scrutiny of a tiny proportion of the European legislation (i.e. the sixty-odd documents which go before the Community's Council of Ministers each month). The existing select committee on European legislation has merely the power to recommend debate on documents which it considers to be of particular importance; and such debates take place either in the standing committee on EC documents (where they attract virtually no attention and rarely last more than half an hour) or in the House itself (where if held at all they take place at 10 p.m. and last for a maximum of an hour and a half). The sum total of Commons scrutiny of European legislation in the 1987/8 session was twenty-four short debates, sixteen of them held after 10 p.m.

---

* MPs themselves now recognise this: a November 1989 poll for Channel Four's *Commons Touch* revealed that an overwhelming majority (87% of the 300 surveyed) believe they had insufficient opportunity to scrutinise European legislation.

* *Ministerial accountability*. Key decisions in the Community are taken by the Council of Ministers and the biannual meetings of heads of government, with individual ministers and prime ministers (or equivalent) accountable to their national parliaments. Yet the instruments possessed by the House of Commons for ensuring the accountability of British ministers are derisory, consisting only of occasional statements after meetings of the Council or heads of government and twice-yearly debates on six-monthly reports on Community affairs, often held months after the period reported. There is not even a separate Question Time slot devoted to European affairs.

* *Weakness of links with the European Parliament*. Parliament has no formal relations with the European Parliament (EP), not even with the members (MEPs) returned for British constituencies. Perversely, as the EP has gained in authority, links between Britain's MPs and MEPs have become ever more attenuated. Before the first direct elections to the EP in 1979, all Britain's MEPs were MPs or peers; since then, links have been preserved only through MEPs with double mandates, and their number has dwindled rapidly (after the 1989 Euro election Britain's eighty-one MEPs included only three peers and two MPs, both of the latter from Northern Ireland). Yet neither the Commons nor the major parties themselves have seriously attempted to foster relations with their MEP colleagues. Indeed, indifference tinged with a jealousy of 'Euro-pretenders' ensured that until recently MEPs were not even allowed their own passes to enter the Palace of Westminster. According to Christopher Prout, leader of Britain's Conservative MEPs, a 'sense of frustration' is keenly felt among MEPs that their expertise and influence are neither valued nor drawn upon at all at Westminster.

However great the chauvinistic feelings of MPs towards their European counterparts, continuing to send them to Coventry is likely to cost the Commons dearly. For under the Single European Act the EP has new powers – under the so-called 'co-operation procedure' – to amend certain types of European legislation, whilst such legislation can then in some cases be passed by the Council of Ministers by a qualified majority vote (i.e. potentially without the consent of British ministers). The details are complex, but the moral is clear: if the Commons hopes to influence EC initiatives and legislation in future it will have *both* to equip itself with effective instruments for influencing British ministers before they participate in the Council of Ministers *and* to build relations – of formal and informal kinds – with the

European Parliament and its members. To enable it to do so, three possible avenues of reform, none mutually exclusive, stand out:

* *A Commons select committee on the EC*. Select committees are likely to be the most effective instruments for developing expertise and channels of influence on Community affairs. But they might take one of a number of forms. The Commons could set up an equivalent of the Lords' European Communities Committee; it could seek to form a joint committee with the Lords; or it could channel scrutiny through the existing DSCs, perhaps by means of special sub-committees. Whatever the structure, a select committee, if effectively organised and serviced, would ensure that a number of MPs would come to give close and fairly continuous attention to Community developments, and the committee would doubtless gain influence over ministers, MEPs and perhaps also the Commission.

* *A grand committee on EC affairs*. Given the pressure of time on the floor of the House, it has been suggested that ministerial account-ability to the Commons could best be improved by the setting up of a grand committee of seventy-odd MPs, on the lines of the Scottish and Welsh GCs, to which ministers would report after – and possibly in some cases before – meetings of the Council of Ministers or heads of government.

* *Improved links with European institutions*. The most efficacious measure for this purpose would be to include MEPs in some or all of the Commons' committees for overseeing European affairs. Indeed, such a move would do more than simply establish links between MEPs and MPs; it would bring expertise and first-hand experience of Brussels directly to bear on Commons' scrutiny and, conversely, give MPs themselves at least an indirect opening to the European Parliament. And lest it be thought an unacceptably radical step, it is worth noting that the Belgian Parliament currently appoints committees composed of equal numbers of its own members and its MEPs for scrutiny purposes, to good effect.

In the light of this critique, the actual recommendations of the Procedure Committee (*The Scrutiny of European Legislation*, 4th report, 1988/9 session) appear grossly inadequate. The committee rejected all proposals for other than minor structural changes. A new European Community select committee was rejected as 'not feasible' in view of the 'time and human resources' required, despite the admission that 'no [existing] committees ... conduct anything approach-ing systematic scrutiny of European legislation'. Similarly, the

Procedure Committee recognised the necessity for the House to develop closer links with the European Parliament, but any form of partici- pation by British MEPs in the proceedings of the Commons and its committees was dismissed as 'a radical, some might say revolutionary, step'. The Procedure Committee merely proposed minor alterations to the existing Standing Committee on European Community Documents and urged existing select committees to pay more heed to Community business.*

Far more ambitious than any of the above ideas, however, is one put forward by the former Conservative Defence Secretary Michael Heseltine, first in his book *The Challenge of Europe* and more fully in a pamphlet published in November 1989. Heseltine proposes the establishment of a second chamber for the European Parliament comprising 152 senators appointed from member Parliaments, including twenty from Britain, charged with reconciling conflicts between national parliaments and the European Parliament. Amend- ments to the Treaty of Rome would be needed before such a European Senate could be set up, though such a step would in any case only make sense in the context of enhanced powers for the European Parliament itself, which could only come from the same process. The proposal represents a bold attempt to reconcile parliamentary control with the reality that much of the effective decision-making power in the Community has already moved to Brussels. And the means of creating such a Senate will soon be at hand with an intergovernmental conference – the forum necessary for agreeing treaty amendments between the Community's member states – likely to begin work in 1991 to provide for the later stages of EMU.

Michael Heseltine's pamphlet is entitled *The Democratic Deficit*. That in itself marks the first recognition by a senior British politician of a theme rehearsed by Community commentators for some years, namely the lack of direct democratic oversight and control over the EC's bureaucracy and decision-making process, and acceptance that the only effective long-term solution lies in an enhanced role for the European Parliament. A European Senate of some kind could make such an outcome more effective, as well as more acceptable to the member states themselves. But it will not come into being in the

* To be fair, it proposed that each select committee should be empowered to up a sub-committee specifically for Community affairs; but discretion as to whether or not to do so is to be left to the individual committees, and it is unlikely that more than a few (if that) will be established.

near future, and until then national parliaments must themselves act to reduce the democratic deficit; indeed, even were the European Parliament strengthened, national parliaments would still have a vital role to play in overseeing the activities of their own ministers in Brussels and in focusing public debate on national — as opposed to European — interests. If the British Parliament is to play any such role, it needs swiftly to redress the democratic deficit at Westminster before its already marginal influence on Community affairs withers on the vine.

Whither Parliament?

'The principal objective of parliamentary activity', the Commons Procedure Committee observed in 1987, 'is to put the politics and actions of Government under close scrutiny.' That is, in fact, a total misconception, for unquestionably the *principal* objective of parliamentary activity is to create and sustain a government, without which there would be no policies and actions to scrutinise in the first place. This inversion is not mere sophistry: it is essential to understanding the dynamics of parliamentary behaviour. And if it is not understood then it is impossible to grasp the problematic inherent in Parliament's *secondary* role as scrutineer — namely, how to exercise oversight and influence whilst sustaining a government, respecting its executive sphere, and submitting to the dictates of party management which make both of the latter possible. Even this formulation is open to criticism, for few MPs so much as pretend to be judge-like scrutineers, whatever the Procedure Committee says. In reality most are pugilistic party politicians, and those calling for a 'redressing of the balance of power between Parliament and the Executive' — the most hackneyed cliché in the reformer's lexicon — can all too often appear oblivious of what the House of Commons actually is: a cohort of ministers and their acolytes on the one hand, of would-be ministers (whether on the Opposition or government back benches) on the other, with only a minority consciously apart from either group.

Most non-ministerial MPs — that is, some four-fifths of the total — do, nonetheless, recognise and perform a scrutiny role, even if only as a by-product of their partisan and constituency endeavours; and recent developments — notably in the House of Lords and in the Commons committee system, combined with the rise of a new generation of full-time and more independent-minded MPs — have served to strengthen the scrutiny process. There is clearly scope for further advances, though short of major external change they will continue to be of an essentially incremental nature. At bottom, however, one factor above all makes parliamentary influence an ongoing reality: the fact that while Parliament does not itself govern, government takes place through Parliament. In this respect, Parliament is akin to the funnel linking a coffee percolator with the jug beneath: decisions and legislation 'brewed' elsewhere have − at least potentially − to pass through it, giving MPs and peers a greater or lesser capacity to modify or restrain them *en route*.

To continue the metaphor, prospective challenges to Parliament's standing look set to take the form of leaks in the percolator resulting in the funnel being bypassed altogether. That done, Parliament's ability to modify and restrain will not only be reduced; its capacity to fulfil Bagehot's 'expressive' function will be limited too.* There is nothing new in such leaks: the quasi-corporatism of the 1960s and 1970s visibly downgraded Parliament even as the *public* forum for national debate. But the leaks of the 1980s and 1990s, notably those springing from Brussels, threaten a significant long-term derogation of parliamentary influence. Sanguine delineations of what might possibly be attained in Utopia are as unattractive to today's MPs as they were to Gladstone; but consideration of attainable and practicable reforms is essential if Parliament is to keep up with the 'acceleration of history'.

---

* It should be stressed that Parliament remains a remarkably effective 'expressive' forum, and is likely to be made more so by televising of the Commons. For all the popular cynicism about politicians, social attitude surveys show a significant increase not only in the readiness of individuals to attempt to influence decisions, but in their perceptions of their ability to do so. And this new-found activity is directed largely at Parliament. Almond and Verba, in their attitudes survey of 1959, found only 6% of respondents who had ever done anything to try to influence Parliament; Anthony Heath's 1986 survey, by contrast, found 44% who reported having done so, and even if the signing of petitions is excluded, 20% still remained. Moreover, half of the 1986 respondents said that if faced with the prospect of an 'unjust or harmful' law they would write to their MP (a positive course of action exceeded only by 'signing a petition'), and one in ten reported actually having done so.

Further reading

This list is intended as a guide to the most useful books and articles.

General

Paul Silk's *How Parliament Works* (Longman, 2nd ed., 1989) and Oonah McDonald's *Parliament at Work* (Methuen, 1989) bring the people and proceedings of the two Houses to life, the first written by a Clerk of the Commons and the second by a former Labour MP.

The House of Commons Public Information Office has published upwards of fifty brief 'factsheets' on most aspects of the structure and business of the Commons. A list of them, and the factsheets themselves, can be procured free of charge by writing to the Public Information office, House of Commons, London SW1A OAA.

The best up-to-date evaluations of Parliament are:

J.A.G. Griffith and Michael Ryle, *Parliament* (Sweet & Maxwell, 1989)

Philip Norton (ed.), *Parliament in the 1980s* (Blackwell, 1985)

Michael Ryle and Peter G. Richards (eds.), *The Commons Under Scrutiny* (Routledge, !988)

David and Gareth Butler's *British Political Facts 1900–1985* (Macmillan, 1986), contains sections on Parliament, elections, governments and parties

Erskine May's *Parliamentary Practice* is the authoritative guide to the practice and procedure of the two Houses. The most recent edition (the 20th, 1983) is edited by Sir Charles Gordon

The Palace of Westminster

Bryan Fell and K. R. MacKenzie, *The Houses of Parliament* (HMSO, 14th ed., 1988). See also:
T. G. B. Cocks, *Mid-Victorian Masterpiece* (Hutchinson, 1977)
Sir Robert Cook, *The Palace of Westminster* (Macmillan, 1987)

Elections

David Butler and Dennis Kavanagh, *The British General Election of 1987* (Macmillan, 1988)
A. Heath, R. Jowell and J. Curtice, *How Britain Votes* (Pergamon, 1985)
Michael Kinnear, *The British Voter: an Atlas and Survey since 1885* (Batsford, 2nd ed., 1981)

MPs

Lisanne Radice, Elizabeth Vallance and Virginia Willis, *Member of Parliament* (Macmillan, 1987) is the best general survey. See also:
David Judge, *Backbench Specialisation in the House of Commons* (Heinemann, 1981)
Peter G. Richards, *The Backbenchers* (Faber, 1974)
Richard Rose, 'British MPs: More Bark than Bite', in E. N. Suleiman (ed.), *Parliaments and Parliamentarians in Democratic Politics* (Holmes and Meier, 1986)
D. D. Searing, 'The role of the good constituency member ... in Great Britain', *Journal of Politics*, 47 (1985)
The Times Guide to the House of Commons, June 1987 (detailed results of the 1987 election in each constituency and biographies of MPs and unsuccessful candidates)
Elizabeth Vallance, *Women in the House* (Athlone Press, 1979)
D. N. Wood, 'The Conservative Member of Parliament as lobbyist for constituency economic interests', *Political Studies*, 35 (1987)

Speaker

P. Laundy, *The Office of Speaker* (Cassell, 1964)
P. Marsden, *The Officers of the Commons* (HMSO, 1979)

Legislation

J. A. G. Griffith, *Parliamentary Scrutiny of Government Bills* (Allen and Unwin, 1974)

See also:

Alf Dubs, *Lobbying: An Insider's Guide to the Parliamentary Process* (Pluto Press, 1989)

D. Englefield, *Whitehall and Westminster* (Longman, 1985)

A. G. Jordan and J. J. Richardson, *Government and Pressure Groups in Britain* (Clarendon, 1987)

David Marsh and Melvyn Read, *Private Members' Bills* (Cambridge University Press, 1988)

Parliament and the Executive (Royal Institute of Public Administration, 1982)

Commons committees

Gavin Drewry (ed.), *The New Select Committees* (Clarendon, 2nd ed., 1989)

Parliament and finance

Sir Leo Pliatzky, *The Treasury under Mrs Thatcher* (Blackwell, 1989)

Ann Robinson, *Parliament and Public Spending* (Heinemann, 1978)

The House of Lords

Donald Shell, *The House of Lords* (Philip Allen, 1988). See also:

Andrew Adonis, 'The House of Lords in the 1980s', *Parliamentary Affairs*, 41, 3 (1988)

Reform and comparative studies

Vernon Bogdanor (ed.), *Representatives of the People?* (Gower, 1985)

K. A. Bradshaw and D. A. M. Pring, *Parliament and Congress* (Quartet, 3rd ed., 1981)

V. Herman, *Parliaments of the World* (Macmillan, 1976)

D. Judge (ed.), *The Politics of Parliamentary Reform* (Heinemann, 1983)

The Final Report of the Labour Policy Review (Labour Party, 1989)

E. N. Suleiman, *Parliaments and Parliamentarians in Democratic Politics* (Holmes and Meier, 1986)

Index